SECRET RITUAL

OF THE

PYTHIAN KNIGHTHOOD

DAMON AND PYTHIAS.

James R. Carnahan

ISBN 1-56459-383-5

PYTHIAN KNIGHTHOOD:
ITS HISTORY AND LITERATURE.

CHAPTER I.

Secret Societies — Two Classes of — Antiquity of — Sought for by Learned Men — The Promoters of Letters, Science, and Art — The Avenues by which the early Christians spread the Gospel — Have Stood the Test of Ages — The Spirit of.

"THERE is nothing new under the sun" is an old saying, and one of much truth. The adage may be applied to secret societies, for it must have been a very early period in the history of man in which they were not found. They came into existence as the natural outgrowth of the social nature of enlightened humanity. We seek companionship not from an artificial culture, but from a natural desire, and so came families, tribes, peoples, nations, banded together for companionship, for strength, for protection, for profit, for culture of mind and soul.

That we may not mislead nor be misunderstood, it may be well to understand what is the true definition of a secret society; for while the number of these organizations is increasing with the growth of civilization, and the wants and necessities of mankind, there are those who oppose them and denounce them. This opposition comes almost wholly from the fact that the objectors do not realize fully what secret societies are, either from a legal stand-point, or from an actual or personal knowledge. They refuse to, or cannot, by their social life and standing, enter within the portals, and be enlightened on the subject.

Secret societies may be divided into two classes:

First, those societies whose secrecy consists in nothing more than methods by which the members may be able to recognize each other, and thus be enabled to contribute to the comfort of those who may need assistance, and aid the truly worthy, who might otherwise be left to suffering and want, and at the same time to protect those whose hearts may be sympathetic from impostors and mercenary persons, who may fear the punishment of the law too much to steal, and yet are not ''too proud to beg.'' In this class of secret societies are taught certain lessons, doctrines, and symbols, which can only be learned or obtained after a process of initiation, and under the promise, or binding obligation, that these mysteries shall not be made known to any who have not passed through the same ordeal and instructions and in the same manner as those who have been initiated. This class of secret societies, with the exception of things here mentioned, has no further private or secret matters from the public. Their membership is published to the world in the processions and parades that are seen on our public streets every day, and in their public acts and declarations throughout the civilized world.

The second class of secret societies are those which, in addition to the secret initiations, and their private manner of recognition, add also a secret doctrine, and an entire secrecy as to the objects and aims of their association; the membership is concealed, the times and places of meeting are kept from the knowledge of all who have not entered into these dark and mysterious bodies.

These secret societies of the second class find no avowed advocates or defenders to-day among law abiding and loyal subjects in any civilized and enlightened country. In the first-named class are found all of the great body of those moral and religious and benevolent secret societies that have come down to us from the early morning of civilization and culture of mankind, or have sprung up from the higher civilization of a more recent date, or have found their birth through the patriotism or philanthropy that finds its highest joy in ministering to the wants of a brother.

These societies seek to enlist the noblest of humanity in their ranks. To this end their times and places of meeting are advertised by magnificent structures. Brick and stone and marble are gathered, and the brightest architectural talent is employed in their arrangement and combination, until the building stands complete in its perfect and pleasing shape to attract the attention and thought and desires of men to learn the inner mysteries of an organization that proclaims only "Peace on earth, and good will to men." Such, too, are the modern as well as the ancient secret societies that have guarded their portals by secret signs and signals, only that their social enjoyment, which is one of the divine gifts to man, may be more fully developed into a purer and more perfect system, without the intrusion into their midst of those who may be so gross in nature and disposition that they would cast a cloud over the otherwise brightness of a social gathering, or mar the pleasure of those whose sympathies are in accord each with the other. These, too, look well to that system of benevolence which is so far-reaching in its aims and purposes that it stretches out its arms to carry the trembling orphan, dries the tears of the widow, supports the tottering steps of the aged, nurses the sick, smooths the way of the dying, and buries the dead, and keeps alive only the good words and deeds of those who have passed beyond the river and rest on the other side. Such societies are secret only in their signs and in the lodge-room. Otherwise, and in so far as the fruits that result from the secret meetings, either by day or by night, in practical exemplification of the tenets and doctrines taught and enforced by obligations or vows about the altar of the lodge or castle hall, these societies are as open and as easy to be observed of all men as the sun at midday. "By their fruits ye shall know them"; fruits that are gathered in a full and abundant harvest.

Secret societies of the second class are such as first sprang up in the Middle Ages, formed for absolutely secret purposes, and, in so far as their designs and purposes have become known, were for unlawful objects and aims, and against the rights of man, and not for his protection and defense, as in the first class of secret societies. The second class, where it has been revealed by subsequent events, was formed for the overthrow of thrones and nations and peoples. The first class has ever taught and proclaimed loyalty to the government under which its votaries found a home. The records of the world show that the second class has found its greatest enjoyment in the torturing of humanity, the groans, the cries, the blood of the oppressed. The societies of the first class have found their chiefest joy, their greatest strength, in relieving suffering and want, in lightening the burdens of the oppressed, in prolonging life instead of shortening it, in lifting men up and not pulling them down, and thus each member, one with the other, finding his greatest ambition and pleasure in striving which shall best work and best serve; and so working and striving they have made the world the brighter, mankind all the happier, and they themselves better by their acts and living.

So those of us who are members of these modern as well as older secret societies, say to those who are not of us, answer the question and answer it truthfully: are there not two classes of secret societies, as here defined; and if we are classed with the first, as we claim to be, then where is the sin; and if the fruits be good and are "for the healing of the nations," as is found in every day's experience, then why not cease condemning, and join in the good work?

These societies of the first class have been tried by all the standards of the world, as men and nations try and test the affairs of men, that is, by what is done for man's betterment and purification, and it has been pronounced "*good.*" And thus will the verdict of the mighty jury stand until time shall be no more.

The Rev. DeWitt Talmage, D. D., certainly one of the greatest divines of this age, on this question of secret societies says: "But I was talking about secret societies. There isn't a day but the question is asked: 'Are the societies which do their work with closed doors, and admit their members by passwords, and who give each other the secret grip, right or wrong?' It all depends whether the object for which they meet is good or bad, and whether they propose to meet the end by lawful or unlawful means. If they come together for purposes of revelry and wassail, or to plot mischief to the state, then with emphasis I say 'No, they are not right.' But if they gather together for the protection of a craft, for the reclamation of inebriates, for the advancement of art and literature, or as mutual benefit societies, to take care of orphans and widows, or to help support men who, through accident or sickness, are no longer able to earn a livelihood, then just as emphatically I say 'Yes.'

"There are secret societies centuries old in this land and in other lands. They have been very largely denounced as demoralizing institutions; but I have hundreds of friends who belong to them who are consecrated men, pillars in churches, examples of piety and virtue. My common sense tells me that those men would not belong to a bad institution. Those are the men I would like to have for my executors, if I am so fortunate as to leave anything for my household when I die. They are the men who I would like to have carry me out to my last resting place when my work is done. They are the men who would be the first to put their foot on anything like iniquity, and I must, as a common sense man, take their testimony in regard to certain institutions rather than the testimony of those who, having been sworn into certain societies, by their attack of them afterward, prove themselves to be perjurers.

"Whose testimony shall I take as a common sense man, standing from the outside? One of the great secret societies that has been largely condemned during the past few years, in 1883, in this country, gave $1,490,000 to take care of the sick. There are other secret societies which have for their foundation good citizenship and the Bible. Some of them have poured a heaven of sunshine and benediction into the houses of the suffering and the poor.

"Of course, there are secret societies and secret societies; but here's a test for them: 'By their fruits ye shall know them.' A bad society makes bad men; a good society makes good men. A bad man will not stay in a good society; a good man will not in a bad society. That is common sense as well as gospel. In most of the secret societies character is the test. The applicant must be a man of good repute. He must possess the best elements of citizenship. Men are social beings. To cry out against it is to cry out against something divinely appointed. Men are by nature gregarious."

The secret societies were the first great schools for the arts and sciences, and in them were taught the principles of architecture. This was especially true among the Chaldeans, the Ethiopians, and the Egyptians. The youth entrusted to their care were taught the mysteries of religion of that day, and whether true or false, they were made the best citizens of their times; but they were required to give their greatest time to architectural designs, and from out the minds of these men came those magnificent temples and palaces, whose ruins alone are sufficient to put to shame the feeble efforts of the artisans of modern days.

It was from these men, who had gained their great knowledge in the secret sessions of their brotherhoods, came the kings, the statesmen, the warriors of ancient Egypt; it was from their skill and by their genius that the land of the Pharaohs yet speaks to-day. It was this class of men that drew away from their homes in search of "more light" the renowned and illustrious men of ancient Greece—her law-givers, her philosophers, her statesmen, her poets, her musicians and historians. Thither went Solon, Pythagoras, Orpheus, Plato, Herodotus, Lycurgus, and others, that they might take upon themselves the vows and be initiated into the mysteries.

These mysteries were passed from father to son, and to those novitiates who were brought in and down from the Egyptian era to the Greeks and the Romans. To the members of these fraternities was given the exclusive building of the temples, and they by law were made a privileged class, free from the burdens of taxation. They had their appointed places of meeting, and at these places they received the candidates for admission into their ranks, and were bound to one another by oath to afford to each other all needed assistance and support. They had their signs of recognition, and their symbols which were to illustrate the principles and doctrines taught. These organizations, fraternities, spread from Rome into the surrounding nations, everywhere carrying with them the arts and sciences, and in that way strengthening each separate people, whether in Italy, France, Belgium, Switzerland, or Britain. They were the aggressive agents of a higher and better civilization. They went with Roman legions in their campaigns. They mapped out the lines of road and superintended their construction; their designs were put into execution in the bridges that spanned the rivers, and they directed and superintended their construction. Wherever they went they carried the higher arts and civilization of the Roman Empire, carrying into nations, with the sword as their protector, the arts, the sciences, and civil law. In the British Isles they found a lodgment early in the Christian era, and here they founded towns and cities.

It was afterward that the early Christian missionaries found their way into these countries through the lodges of these fraternities, and under their care and protection that the gospel was first preached in Britain, and was preserved in that country when in all others it seemed to have gone out in darkness.

It was through these fraternities that the cities were rebuilt after the invasion of the Danes in the ninth century. But why add further words? The history of the world has been written by these fraternities. Their cultivation of the arts and sciences, the fostering care given by them to letters and literature, the protection vouchsafed by them to the early Christians, has transformed the world from a wild waste to one of beauty, comfort, and joy.

So then, as the friend and defender, the founder and propagator of the arts and the sciences, the supporter of the Christian believer, and the preserver of Christianity, the fraternities, secret societies, ARE *good*.

Let us apply another test, and try secret societies from that stand-point. "Time proves all things." By this test we, who are friends and members of secret societies, are willing that they shall be tried. By this trial He who "spake as never man spake" taught the multitudes that gathered on the plains and mountain sides, by the rivers and on the shores of the lakes of Judea, listening to his words of wisdom as He advised them, to prove all things whether they were true or false, human or divine, the trial by long life, permanency. And so we now challenge those who find fault, who criticise, who denounce secret societies as immoral and unholy in their tendencies, and we say to them if they be not of God, for good, why is it that through all the years of persecution and of trial by fire and sword, by scourgings and torturings, by burnings and death, they have not been everlastingly destroyed and blotted out of existence? Why is it that from the days of Zoroaster, 2000 B. C., these secret societies have lived and flourished? True, their votaries were driven from their homes, and were forced to flee to the mountains and dens and caves of the earth, but they came forth after each period of persecution only to take a firmer hold on the hearts of men.

I think we may find that one great cause for the early establishment of secret societies among men was and is the inherent belief in a higher power than man, the spiritual striving for a higher and purer life. So we find the ancient secret societies were formed for moral and religious training; such were what is known as the "Ancient Mysteries," whose object was, by their initiations to cultivate a purer worship than the popular one. Each of those organizations or bodies, whether gathered about Pythagoras or Plato, found a God to worship; not one of their own class, nor fashioned by human hands, but one who to them was King of Kings and Lord of Lords. A faith in a God whom they believed to be endowed with omniscience, omnipotence and omnipresence, was the central point in all their universe of thought and desire. Such were the schools—societies of the old philosophers. Antedating the Jewish religion, the Supreme Being that was made the central figure in the teaching of Zoroaster was identical with the Jewish idea or conception of Jehovah. He is called the "Creator of the earthly and spiritual life, the Lord of the whole universe, at whose hands are all the creatures." They taught that "He is wisdom and intellect; the light itself and the source of light; the rewarder of the virtuous, and the punisher of the wicked." These societies, long before Judaism had its birth, taught the idea of a future life and the immortality of the soul. Here too was first taught the doctrine of the resurrection of the body, and an eternal existence in a heaven or a hell. The heaven was called the "house of hymns, because the angels sang hymns there." In these beliefs have all the secret societies of what we have termed the first class been formed from their earliest advent until the present time.

In these beliefs, which to-day are the beliefs of the entire Christian world, is found our first answer to the question why secret societies have lived and do live, spite of the persecutions that have come upon them. It is the God in man that makes and gives them life. As it has been in the past, as to their life and growth, so it will be in the future, only that they will come into greater and broader fields, and the light that lights their pathway will grow more and more until it comes to the perfect day of spiritual light and knowledge.

Not only have these societies made the belief in a Divine Creator—God—one of the chief stones in the building, but from the earliest time in their existence have they believed in the brotherhood of man—one common family, with rights and powers inherent in each, and which should be respected by each and all. This was and is a doctrine that has been difficult to establish in its broadest and fullest sense among men. While all to-day admit it to be the proper basis on which all society should rest, yet the history of every-day life in this the closing of the nineteenth century, as in the early ages, points to man's inhumanity toward his fellows, and wrong and oppression sit in high places. Some there always have been who have respected the rights of others; some who, long before the Christian era, tried to practice themselves and inculcate in others the practice of the great commandment: " Whatsoever ye would that men should do unto you, do ye even so to them."

The founders of these societies taught the disciples that gathered about their feet to respect the rights, the property, the lives of their fellow men as those of brothers.

In furtherance of these ends and objects they taught a life of morality, honor, and purity. Through these societies the teaching of a better temporal life grew and developed, until the ushering in of the Christian era, and mankind heard the dual command which to-day is sounding on land and sea, in the palaces of the rich and the homes of the lowly; the command that stands out in characters of light in every fraternal secret society that has existence: "Thou shalt love the Lord thy God with all thy heart and with all thy soul and with all thy mind," and "Thou shalt love thy neighbor as thyself."

These principles of brotherhood, as taught by our fraternal organizations, are most beautifully set forth by a celebrated writer—Cole, and he sums them up as follows:

"First. When the necessities of a brother call for my aid and support, I will be ever ready to lend him such assistance, to save him from sinking, as may not be detrimental to myself or connections, if I find him worthy thereof.

"Second. Indolence shall not cause my footsteps to halt, nor wrath turn them aside; but forgetting every selfish consideration, I will be ever swift of foot to serve, help and execute benevolence to a fellow creature in distress.

"Third. When I offer up my ejaculations to Almighty, God, a brother's welfare I will remember as my own; for as the voices of babes and sucklings ascend to the Throne of Grace, so most assuredly will the breathings of a fervent heart arise to the mansions of bliss, as our prayers are certainly required of each other.

"Fourth. A brother's secrets delivered to me as such, I will keep as I would my own; as betraying that trust might be doing him the greatest injury he could sustain in this mortal life; nay, it would be like the villainy of an assassin, who lurks in darkness to stab his adversary, when unarmed and least prepared to meet an enemy.

"Fifth. A brother's character I will support in his

absence as I would in his presence; I will not wrongfully revile him myself, nor will I suffer it to be done by others, if in my power to prevent it."

So we of the brotherhood, whether as Masons, as Odd Fellows, as Knights of Pythias, and all other kindred bodies, meet and worship at one common altar and adore the Creator of the Universe. In the light of His spirit of love we greet mankind as brothers, and pledge ourselves to one another's up-building. About the altars of the mystic brotherhood, in all ages and in all climes, we have found and seen a spirit of love that brings a feeling of kinship which drives out selfish pride and hate, and helps us to bear one another's burdens.

Within our temple science has found a home, and from thence was knowledge sent that strengthened man for his labors here on earth, and lighted his pathway to the eternal beyond. From these sanctuaries, whether constructed as they often were in mountain fastnesses, or in the groves, God's first temples, or on the open plain, with only the star-lit heavens overhead, have gone those teachings of a higher morality which have made men cleaner and purer in body and mind. To mankind these orders, societies, have been a light when all else was moral darkness; have brought hope when despair had well-nigh possessed the soul; have made men stronger for the struggles through which they have had to pass.

Now, in view of the great good they have done in the past, of the good they are now doing throughout the civilized world, and of the much greater good that they may accomplish in this and the coming eras of increasing knowledge, we say to all fraternal and benevolent societies of the present, and, if it were possible, to all of the future—all hail!

HARBOR OF SYRACUSE,

SHOWING ANCIENT MOLE CONSTRUCTED BY DIONYSIUS

CHAPTER II.

Sicily and the Grecian Period—Syracuse—The Home of Culture and Wealth—Political Condition of Syracuse—The Reign of Gelon—Syracuse as a Democracy—Dionysius, the Tyrant—How he came into Power—His Wars with the Carthaginians—Tyranny and Tyrants—Review of the Life of Dionysius.

EACH SOCIETY, or order, has its great ideals, or prototypes, in human life, in whose deeds they have found traits worthy of emulation. Before coming to the consideration of the life and character of the great prototypes of the Order of Knights of Pythias we should look into the history of the country that was their home, see the men who surrounded them, know something of the customs, the laws, the society by which they were environed. Men do not make themselves; their characters are their own by nature; but these may be moulded and shaped for good or for evil—may be led into honorable lives or to dishonor, according to the surroundings. Here and there are men who have risen above the social influences that were brought to bear upon them, but these are the exceptions in man's history; and, as we shall see further on, Damon and Pythias were exceptions to the rule in their day. Not only do men aid in forming or shaping the characters of their fellow men, but this is also done by the natural surroundings of men. The sky, the rugged mountain peaks, the ocean in all its mighty power beating on the shore, the valley and plain, the river and lake, are all so many educators or fashioners of the lives and characters of men. This has been true of all nations in all ages past; it will be true to a greater or less degree in all time to come. So then let us view first the home of Damon and Pythias, and then the men and people with whom they were brought in contact in their every-day lives.

Sicily is the largest and most beautiful island in the Mediterranean Sea; an island of mountain and plain, full of all that is picturesque in nature, with charms peculiar to itself, so rich, so beautiful, so grand that they outshine the land whose beauties have been so much praised by poet, and so fully sketched by artist, the far-famed Italy.

So bountifully was it provided by nature with herbage and flowers that the ancients claimed that the oxen of the Sun pastured in its rich fields. It was the home of the olive and grape. It was first occupied by the early shepherds, who took possession of it, and finally erected for themselves permanent homes and built cities. Other peoples and nations, attracted by the climate and soil, gradually found a home on its shores. The Cretans, the Trojans, the Phœnicans, all obtained a footing on the island, until it grew to be inhabited by strong and powerful tribes or separate nations.

The Grecian period was the most renowned of all the annals of Sicily. The Greeks, with their learning and culture in letters and science, in art and architecture, finding themselves hemmed in, and their powers abridged within their own boundaries, sought for themselves different fields and greater scope for their genius, and from their wanderings found homes on different parts of the island and along the peninsula, and wherever they stopped they laid the foundations for cities and as many and different and separate states. Some Athenians, the earliest of the Grecian colonies, built Naxos 735 B. C.

The Corinthians and Dorians in their travels came to and landed on the island of Ortygia, there finding the Seculi, drove them out, took possession and laid out and commenced the building of the future home of Damon and Pythias, the city of Syracuse, B. C. 734. And so one after the other the native tribes were driven out and away from the shores and into the mountain fastnesses.

Grecian art, science, and culture, every thing that had made Greece famous up to that period, and has ever kept her name high on the roll of fame, were transplanted to the different cities of Sicily. Magnificent temples were built, costly and elegant palaces were erected, and their ruins to-day attract the attention and admiration of the civilized world. These cities, and notably amongst them Syracuse, became the homes of the learned men of all countries. The painter found employment for his genius, the philosopher gathered about him the youth to learn wisdom; poetry was encouraged, and literary contests brought together men of giant intellects; the soldier was taught all the art of war, and the statesman and jurist were received with marked respect and honor. A noble strife was engendered between the different cities, and Syracuse in all these battles of intellect and genius stood in the front rank. The great Grecian games were also carried into Sicily, and to witness them came fair women and brave men from all shores and nations. Great wealth and treasure had, through commerce and the home industries, accumulated in Syracuse; the supply of gold and silver and precious stones had flowed into the hands of her citizens until this great wealth was now tempting the cupidity of the other nations.

Each of these cities was at first independent in its organization, and possessed a democratic form of government. With the increase and growth in the material wealth and strength of the land came finally discord and dissensions. Ambitious and unprincipled men sowed discord among the people, until internal strife broke out; and, through intrigue and deceit, men who sought their own advancement rather than the good of the people, succeeded in overthrowing the government ''of the people, by the people, and for the people,'' and in its stead established a monarchy and despotism. These in turn were borne by the people until forbearance ceased to be a virtue, and some leader of the people was found who, by his force of character, could and did control and lead the people until the despot was overthrown, and a democratic form of government would be again established. So on through the years and centuries Sicily was one of the world's great battle fields; here was waged the struggle for right against wrong, the oppressed against the oppressor, until the principle of honor and loyalty *seemed* to be lost; and it *was*, as to the great mass of the people. Wars of the greatest magnitude had swept over the land of Sicily. The most powerful army that the Athenians could muster had been sent against Syracuse; the Carthaginians invaded the city by land and by sea with immense fleets and armies, yet all these invaders were driven out and the city and kingdom maintained. Not only in defensive but in aggressive warfare were the Sicilian armies triumphant. Such was ancient Sicily prior to and including the period in which Damon and Pythias are brought to notice.

Let us now take a more careful glance at Syracuse and the tyrant Dionysius, that we may the more fully understand the great underlying principles on which our Order is based. Syracuse, anciently the most famous and powerful city of Sicily, situated on the south-eastern coast of the island, eighty miles southwest of Messina, was founded by a body of Corinthian settlers under Archias, one of the Bacchiadæ, in the year 734 B. C. The original colonists at first occupied nothing more than the little isle of Ortygia, about one mile long and a half mile broad, which lies near the shore. This colony grew rapidly in population and strength, and was enabled to establish subcolonies of its own.

SYRACUSE.

Nothing is definitely known of the early political state of Syracuse; but before 486 B. C. the political power had passed into the hands of a few leading families, or, as they might more properly be termed, clans, who constituted an oligarchy, while the greater part of the citizens formed a malcontent democracy. The oligarchic citizens or families, probably the descendants of the original founders of the city, were expelled, and the sovereign power was transferred to the citizens at large, forming a democratic form of government. Before a year had passed, however, Gelon, despot of Gela, 480 B. C., had restored the exiles, and at the same time had made himself master of Syracuse. He was a great ruler, and under him the city increased in strength and great wealth. It was under the rule of Gelon that the city attained its greatest prosperity and renown. Although besieged by the immense army of the Carthaginians, the Syracusan army, under the command of Gelon, routed the invaders, and Gelon permitted the defeated and captured Carthaginians to return to their homes, fixing only two conditions in the terms of peace: that they should send him two vessels as a token of their gratitude, and the other that they should abolish the custom of sacrificing human beings to Neptune. "This treaty of peace," says a celebrated writer, "was the noblest of any recorded in history. Gelon, after having defeated an army of three hundred thousand Carthaginians, imposes a condition useful to themselves and in behalf of humanity at large." The Syracusans showed their gratitude by raising Gelon to the supreme and sovereign power. He appeared before the council unarmed, his person invested in a cloak, in order, as he said, that any one might slay him who could truthfully show that he had ever been false to a trust, or had done any injury to his country.

Raised to the position of king by the voice of the people, he ruled in justice, and by his genius advanced all the material interests of the city. At his death he was deified by the people whom he had served so faithfully and well.

Although torn at times by factions and internal strife, Syracuse continued to increase in power and wealth to such an extent that a peaceful contest arose between her and the neighboring cities as to which should carry the arts and sciences to the highest state of perfection. The Syracusans outstripped all their rivals, and attained such strength that they were considering the subjugation of all Sicily. They were at this period attacked by an immense army of Athenians, but these were also vanquished, and again came another invasion by the Carthaginians. This brings us now to the period in her history of interest to the members of our Order. Her government had changed from time to time from a monarchy to a democratic form of government, and then again to a monarchy, and so from one to the other as it suited the will or caprice of the people or the intrigues of ambitious men. At the time Dionysius is brought to our notice Syracuse was a democracy. To understand the position in which our prototypes were situated as citizens of Syracuse, we should understand what a democratic government meant in that day. Under it all men enjoyed political rights, and were given the right of suffrage. With their universal suffrage every citizen had a part in the affairs of state; he helped to elect magistrates, became a law-maker, performed duty as jurist and juror; he had a voice in declaring war, or making terms of peace. Although there were great numbers and classes of officials, there was always a distinction kept between the civil power and the military, so that there should be no danger, as was supposed, of having the civil government overthrown by the military.

Of the civil powers there were, first, the magistrates, elected by the votes of the people for a term of one year. To be elected a magistrate secured for that official the utmost respect of the people, for the reason that having by their votes elected him he was considered a part of themselves, and to despise him was to despise themselves. Suffrage was one of the most sacred sources of authority.

Higher than the magistrates, whose duty it was to administer and enforce the laws, was the senate. This was a deliberative body, a council of state; it made no laws, repealed no laws, exercised no sovereignty. This body was composed of a certain number from each tribe or class, who performed their sacred duties in rotation, and deliberated all the year round upon the religious and political interests of the city.

Above the senate was the assembly of the people. Here was the real, controlling power, the sovereignty. The conventions of the assembly were always held in some sacred enclosure. The people were seated on stone benches. An altar stood near the speaker's stand, and the stand itself was considered as sacred as an altar. Religious rites were performed and prayers were offered. This was one of the prayers always to be offered: '' We invoke the gods that they may protect the city. May the advice of the wisest prevail. Cursed be he who shall give us bad counsel; who shall attempt to change the decrees and the law, or who shall reveal our secrets to the enemy.''

Then a herald, under instruction of the president, announced the subject for which the assembly had been convened. Before this meeting had been convened, the subject had been discussed and considered by the senate. It was the duty of the senate to formulate the laws or decrees, and submit them to the assembly, and no other question or law could be taken up or discussed save that for which the assembly was called, and the act or statute presented could be adopted or rejected. By the proclamation of the herald an opportunity was given for those who wished, to speak. They prized their orators, and always gave them attention, yet all good citizens were privileged to speak. It is said that there was a law that punished every orator who was convicted of having given bad advice to the people, and any speaker who had three times advised resolutions contrary to existing laws was forbidden to speak. These people realized fully that a strict observance of the law was their only safety. It was required that all propositions for changing the laws must first be presented to the senate, where, after due consideration, they were rejected or approved. If rejected, that was the end of it; but if the proposed measure was approved by a vote of their body, then the senate convened the assembly, where it was discussed, and submitted for action to a commission selected by the assembly; if this commission rejected it, their decision was final; if, however, they approved it, then the assembly was reconvened, the measure voted on, and could there be rejected or, by their votes, become a law. Every man was made personally responsible for his vote, and no one was permitted to evade the consequences of his acts.

We have dwelt thus long on the democracy of the days of Damon and Pythias that it might be the more fully understood how heinous the offense that was committed by Dionysius and his co-conspirators appeared in the eyes of Damon, the senator, and it was his loyalty to his city and nation that brought upon him the condemnation of the tyrant, and brought to his side the courageous and steadfast friend, the soldier and valiant Knight, Pythias.

Just at the time when this democratic form of government was the strongest, the island of Sicily was again overrun with the Carthaginians, and Dionysius appeared on the stage of action, and here we take up a sketch of his life.

Dionysius the Elder, tyrant of Syracuse, was born 430 or 431 B. C. He was originally a clerk in a public office, but manifested at an early age a passion for political and military distinction.

THE TYRANT DIONYSIUS.

When the Argentines, after the conquest of their city by the Carthaginians, accused the Syracusan generals, who had failed to relieve them, of treachery, Dionysius supported their accusations before the people of Syracuse, and induced the latter to appoint new commanders for the army, and so contrived that he himself was selected as one of the number. In a short time he supplanted his colleagues also, and, when only twenty-five years of age, made himself, by the help of his mercenaries, absolute ruler of the city. To strengthen his tyranny he married the daughter of Hermocrates, the late head of the aristocratic party in Syracuse, and thus attached the followers of that leader to himself.

After he had fiercely suppressed several insurrections against himself and his tyrannous government, and had conquered some of the Greek towns of Sicily, he made great preparations for a war against the Carthaginians. This war began in the year 397 B. C.

At first fortune favored Dionysius, but after a short period he suffered a series of reverses so calamitous that the greater portion of his allies abandoned him, and he was shut up in the city of Syracuse, apparently without any hope of release or escape.

During this siege the better class of the people of Syracuse, who had been robbed of their property, and had suffered in divers ways by and through the tyrant Dionysius, and now once more having arms in their hands for the common defense of their city, and believing that the time had come to throw off the yoke of the tyrant, began openly to proclaim their discontent. In order to quiet this threatened outbreak, and not daring to attempt to suppress it by arms, Dionysius convened a public assembly. At or near the close of the assembly, the historian tells us that one Theodorus, a Horseman, or Knight, a person of wealth and station, of high character and well-known reputation for courage, rose and addressed the assembly.

His arraignment of Dionysius furnishes in a short space the most complete review of the life and character of that ruler, and we give here the conclusion of the address. Having reviewed at length the career of the tyrant, he appeals to the Syracusans:

"Dionysius [he said] is a worse enemy than the Carthaginians, who, if victorious, would be satisfied with a regular tribute, leaving us to enjoy our properties and our paternal polity. Dionysius has robbed us of both. He has pillaged our temples of their sacred deposits. He has slain or banished our wealthy citizens, and then seized their properties by wholesale, to be transferred to his satellites. He has given the wives of these exiles in marriage to his barbarian soldiers. He has liberated our slaves, and taken them into his pay in order to keep their masters in slavery; has garrisoned our city against us by means of these slaves, together with a host of other mercenaries. He has put to death every citizen who ventured to raise his voice in defense of the laws and constitution. He has abused our confidence—once, unfortunately, carried so far as to nominate him general—by employing his powers to subvert our freedom, and rule us according to his selfish rapacity, in place of justice. He has further stripped us of our arms; these, recent necessity compelled him to restore, and these, if we are men, we shall now employ for the recovery of our freedom."

He then reviews the war in which they were engaged, and charges Dionysius with disgraceful incompetence, and concludes:

" Let us look for another leader, in place of a sacreligious temple-robber whom the gods have now abandoned. If Dionysius will consent to relinquish his dominion, let him retire from the city with his property unmolested; if he will not, we are here assembled, we are possessed of our arms, and we have both Italian and Peloponnesian allies by our side. The assembly will decide whether it will choose leaders from our own citizens, or from our metropolis, Corinth, or from the Spartans, the presidents of all Greece."

As bitter and as fierce as had been the denunciation, and although the native Syracusans were ready, if aided, to answer the call of the orator, yet they were doomed to disappointment, for the allies on which they had reckoned took sides with Dionysius, and he held his position. Just at this juncture, too, the fortunes of war turned to his advantage.

When he had well-nigh despaired of saving the city from capture by the Carthaginian army and navy, that was then almost surrounding it by land and sea, and it seemed as though there was to be no possible escape for himself, either from the enemy on the outside, or the wrath of the Syracusans within, a terrible pestilence broke out in the Carthaginian army and fleet. This epidemic the tyrant was quick to perceive could be turned to his advantage every way. The people of that day were superstitious. Their gods were many and their temples were sacred, and iconoclasm in their minds was sure to meet the vengeance of the outraged gods. Imilkon, the Carthaginian general, had pillaged the temples of two of their gods, and so Dionysius appealed to the piety of the citizens of Syracuse, and interpreted the pestilence now ravaging the ranks of their enemies as the avenging wrath of the gods, because of the desecration of the temples, and thus incited them once more to rally around his standards by claiming that the gods, by thus avenging the affront to them, would further avenge it by helping him to utterly destroy their enemy and the enemy of their gods.

Dionysius was also quick to see that the pestilence was to be to him a greater ally than all of the allies who had abandoned him could possibly have been had they remained with him, and the pestilence had not broken out in the camps and ships of the besieging hosts. He saw in this calamity to his enemies an opportunity for the success of his arms, and he immediately attacked the foe by land and by sea in such sudden and fierce manner that he not only raised the siege, but almost utterly destroyed the Carthaginian army.

But even in this victory he displayed his utter baseness and bloodthirsty spirit, for he so planned that the citizens of Syracuse, who had desired his removal, should be destroyed, although they were in the line and engaged with the army in action, and he so arranged that in the midst of the battle on a certain portion of the line his mercenaries should suddenly abandon the field, and thus their comrades, being deserted, would be cut to pieces by the Carthaginians. This plan was fully carried out, and the men who had helped to save Syracuse, and the life of the tyrant himself, were ruthlessly slain.

So great a success over the enemies of Syracuse once more fully established Dionysius in his place as ruler, and put down all the opposition that had been manifested against him during the siege.

Twice after this the Carthagenians renewed their hostilities against Syracuse, but both times they were sorely defeated, and Dionysius was enabled to conclude a most advantageous peace both for himself and his people.

Dionysius now turned his arms against Lower Italy, and although stoutly resisted on all sides, his armies, under his leadership, met with ultimate success in whatever direction they turned their faces. He stood as the greatest military chieftain of his age, having under his command larger and more thoroughly equipped armies than had ever before been brought together, the number of his soldiers running up into the hundreds of thousands, while his fleets swept the Tyrrhenian and Adriatic seas.

Toward the close of his life, however, he met with some reverses in his military career, but none that seriously weakened or impaired his power. His was a peculiar talent,

ANCIENT QUARRIES NEAR SYRACUSE.

EAR OF DIONYSIUS.

strong in intellect, and possessed of wonderful power and ability to quickly perceive those peculiarly fortunate opportunities that rarely come to a man twice in his life-time, he grasped and held everything that would in the least indicate the smile of fortune, and wrested from it wealth and power and fame. That he was cruel in the highest degree cannot be denied; that his was an ambition for the most part unholy and selfish in the extreme is undoubtedly true; yet that there were many circumstances to make him the man he became is equally true; and that he had some good in him is abundantly proven. Now let us briefly consider what his surroundings were, what he accomplished for Syracuse, and also notice his achievements in time of peace.

We, as members of the Order of Knights of Pythias, hear much said of the *tyrant* Dionysius, and, from what is oft repeated, despise him in our love for our prototypes, Damon and Pythias. Yet from what may be learned of him he was a most extraordinary man, and we may look to his surroundings somewhat, and then perhaps judge him less harshly because of his kindness to the two friends whom he had so thoroughly tested, doubting that there was any true and firm friendship in the face of death, and for whom after the test he had so much admiration.

To judge of tyranny or tyrants in the time of ancient Syracuse, let us first ascertain, if possible, what was understood by the name tyrant, or term tyranny, by the Syracusans. In every city then, as now, two great forces existed, always to a greater or less degree enemies to each other, and both striving for the mastery—the *rich* and the *poor*.

At that time there was no opportunity for the poor to better their condition except by despoiling the rich. The rich were put upon the defensive at all times in order to protect and preserve their property. The democracy were the rich and powerful. They were the men who bore arms, or had the right to bear arms as soldiers. Whenever there was a civil war it was of that cruel and relentless kind that comes from cupidity on the part of the poor on one side, and from the hatred of the poor by the rich on the other.

Aristotle says the rich took this oath among themselves: "I swear always to remain the enemy of the people, and to do them all the injury in my power."

The rich were the cultivated and enlightened classes. They understood and appreciated the value of a democratic form of government, such as has been before described; they felt the necessity of preserving such a form of government, and thus holding their property free from a *tyranny* which meant the right of the tyrant to despoil them, in order to distribute to the poor, and thereby enable him to gain and hold them for his defense.

The poor, in their struggles for life, seeing the outward pleasure and display of the rich, thoughtless of their few political rights, and desiring rather their own aggrandizement, were ever ready to join together under some one who had shown his power and ability as a leader, and overthrow the democracy, establish a monarchy, and place the power in the hands of a tyrant, who would be willing to divide the wealth of the land in order to hold his place.

Says one of our historians, in writing of that time, "*Liberty* signified the government where the rich had the rule, and defended their fortunes; tyranny indicated exactly the contrary." So the tyrant was he who was the choice of the people, the populace.

Says Aristotle, "The mission of the tyrant is to protect the people against the rich; he has always commenced by being the demagogue, and it is the essence of tyranny to oppose the aristocracy. The means of arriving at a tyranny is to gain the confidence of the multitude, and one does this by declaring himself the enemy of the rich. This was the course of Piesistratus at Athens, of Theagenes at Megara, and of Dionysius at Syracuse."

The historian Grote most graphically describes Dionysius in his harangue before the assembly after the fall of Agrigentum, as he denounced the Syracusan generals. He set himself in defiance of the magistrates, and by them was fined for disorder, but this was paid by his supporters. He denounced not only the generals, but also the conspicuous and wealthy citizens generally, "as oligarchs who held tyrannical sway." "Syracuse [he contended] could not be saved, unless men of a totally different character were invested with authority; men not chosen from wealth and station, but of humble birth, belonging to the people by position." Demagogism was as great in that day as at the present time.

Raised to power by this worst element of society, in a time when there was but little of moral teaching, and the passions of men were easily inflamed, the tyrant was in the power of the mob. The force that made him tyrant did it to gratify their desire for the property of others, and he knew that from time to time, as their greed demanded it, he must despoil the rich to minister to the demands of the baser portion of his subjects, or his power would depart from him forever. The life of men weighed for naught as against the desire to maintain power. The power of the tyrant was circumscribed by no law that he was bound to respect. The subject had no rights which might conflict with the tyrant's desire or ambition. He knew, also, that in the midst of his power he was not safe from the hand of the avenger, nor free from the knife of the assassin. The friend of to-day was one who to-morrow would shout "The king is dead, long live the king," as a new tyrant would take his place. Flattery was one of the corner-stones on which the tyrant of Syracuse must build his throne, and that was flattery of the worst elements of the city. Such was the state of society, or government, in that day, that when the tyrant came in, all safety for individual men went out; ownership in property existed only till the tyrant saw fit to take it; there was no way whereby the citizen could protect himself from his caprice or cruelty; he held the life, the property, every thing there was of the citizen, in his grasp.

Such, briefly stated, was the tyrant; and such the tyranny of Dionysius, in the days of Damon and Pythias. Aside from the question of his life as a tyrant, what can be said? No man of his time had a greater diversity of power. He was a statesman of no mean ability. He was the greatest warrior and soldier of his age. While he was cruel in his treatment of his subjects at times, as all tyrants were, yet he had much in his nature that was princely and generous. While he was ambitious to be considered the greatest ruler of all in that day, he was not content with his reputation as a statesman or a soldier. He turned his attention to literary pursuits. While he pandered to the mob on one hand, on the other he gathered about himself the learned, the students, the poets, and the philosophers of his period from all the Grecian cities. Plato was said to have been his guest, brought to his court by special invitation. He studied, he wrote, until finally he entered the lists as a contestant for literary and poetic honors. He strove for the honors, and for the prize in the Olympic games, and in the year 388 B. C. he sent his literary productions to Athens, the most renowned city of the enlightened world, and with them an influential embassy to press his claims. Although he failed in this first effort, he did not retire from the literary arena; but, in the intervals between the numerous wars, prosecuted his studies, and by all the aids he could bring to his assistance kept alive the desire to win the highest honors in the world of letters, and, on several occasions, in spite of the bitter prejudice that existed against him, carried off the second and third prizes for tragedy.

The wars with his old Carthaginian enemies were kept up

ANCIENT GREEK THEATER NEAR SYRACUSE.

with varying success until about the year 383 or 382 B. C.,
when the fortunes of Dionysius left him, and he was most
signally defeated by the Carthaginians, and in one day he
was reduced from the position of one who dictates terms
of peace to that of one who is willing to accept any terms,
so that life is spared.   He then for a number of years remained in quiet.   During this period of quietude we only
know of him as a student gathering about him men of
letters, and still further engaged in building walls of protection and defense about the city of Syracuse, and in
beautifying the city.   About the year 370 B. C. he had
sufficiently recovered from the disaster of his defeat, and
again found a pretext for war upon the Carthaginian
provinces in Sicily, and sought to expel them, the Carthaginians, entirely from Sicily.   After he had made a demand upon them for a complete evacuation of Sicilian territory, which they refused, or rather received and treated
the demand with silent contempt, he gave battle and
succeeded in part in recovering the territory that had
been held by the Carthaginians.   It was while engaged in
this campaign, which proved to be his last, that he received
the intelligence that he had been successful in the contest
he had been so long waging in the field of letters.   He
had been awarded first honors for one of his tragedies at
the Lenaean festival of Athens.   Long had he been the
first military hero until forced into a temporary retirement,
which had evidently been to him "a blessing in disguise,"
for now, when his military star was again in the ascendant,
his fondest hopes were fully realized, and he was now to
wear the laurel for a victory that was won without being
stained by the blood of his fellow man.   But while he had
been able to wear the soldier's wreath of victory with dignity, and without dissipation or undue manifestations of
joy, the news of his peaceful victory at Athens led him
into great excess of feasting and drinking.   Sacrifices and

thank-offerings were offered to the gods, and great was the revelry, and, it might be said, debauch.

From this dissipation he never recovered, as a fever set in, and in a short time he died, before he had accomplished his purpose of expelling the Carthaginians. It was believed by many that his death was brought about by his physicians, through the instigation of his son, thus furnishing another illustration of the instability and uncertainty of the power of a tyrant. For thirty-eight years he had held Sicily in his grasp, proof against all the combinations that had been formed by his countrymen for his overthrow and the release of the land from his bloody hand, and the more cruel outrages of the mercenary hordes by which he was enabled to hold his people. For thirty-eight years after Damon and Pythias had refused his friendship he had lived with only such friends, so-called, as could be purchased by the wealth that had been filched from honest citizens to be bestowed upon those who were his willing tools in crime. He was a most vigorous ruler in every respect; he built up the material wealth of the cities of Sicily over which he ruled by despoiling others. He was ambitious, and was estopped by no conscientious convictions of right or wrong in the pursuit of any object that might serve his purposes or secure the ends he sought. While he beautified and adorned Syracuse, he did it over the ruined homes, and by the banishment, plundering, and slaying of her best citizens to gratify his own ambition. Soldier he was, but hero he was not, for the soldier-hero is one who is courageous and daring as was Dionysius, but in victory he is magnanimous and kind to the vanquished. Dionysius was cruel and blood-thirsty, therefore he should be classed as the enemy of good government and humanity. He was strong in mind and of brilliant intellect, as his literary victories show; but, like Lady Macbeth, he could never rid his mind and vision of the blood spot, and in the last years of his life he was continually tormented with the belief that he was shadowed by those who were seeking his life to avenge the death of the many whom he had slain. To-day his literary and peaceful victories are over-shadowed by the record he made as an enemy of mankind; his skill and renown as chieftain is tarnished by the pages of bloody history he made, which showed that he was devoid of the high and noble qualities of a true soldier. The great mass of history he made is a blot on the world's pages.

It will now be pleasant to turn away from the brief review of this man's life, which was a life devoid of the sunshine of friendship, and take up the lives of the two men who stand to-day as exemplars of all that is brave, and loyal, and true; true to their country, true to one another, and true to the noble and unselfish part of humanity. How great a difference there was between the life of Dionysius, the tyrant, and those of the noble senator of Syracuse, Damon, and the true soldier, the tried and faithful friend, Pythias, is best shown in the drama which was made the foundation for the ritual and tenets of our Order, for it was from this that the inspiration was drawn which produced the ritual. However, before producing the drama let us understand and know something of these two characters. This we will do in the next chapter—the historic **Damon** and Pythias.

CHAPTER III.

THE HISTORIC DAMON AND PYTHIAS.

THE story of Damon and Pythias a fabrication, as some have claimed, or were they actual characters in the world's great drama? The characters borne by them, or rather given to them, in the popular drama which bears their names, have been looked upon by many as the fruit of the vivid imagination of the author, and we find more than one Dionysius who is not willing to admit that such friendship, such fidelity and loyalty could be shown by one human being to another. That the two men, Damon and Pythias, did live, that they were the steadfast friends that they are represented to have been, cannot be doubted in the light of history.

An earnest Pythian of modern days, one who has achieved the highest honors that can be conferred upon him in his own Grand Jurisdiction, has gone most thoroughly into the study of ancient literature and history to settle the disputed question, desiring to give to the Order the very best authenticated history of the prototypes of Pythian Knighthood. This honorable and scholarly Knight has furnished the result of his investigations for publication in this work, and we are glad to give these researches to the world through the medium of this book, not alone for its historical worth, but to show to men of literary and scholastic attainments the class of men, intellectual men, that are now taking an interest in the Order of Knights of Pythias, and we therefore produce these translations from the old authors and historians, as a part of our Pythian literature.

The author of these translations is the Hon. Charles Cowley, LL. D., of Lowell, Massachusetts. Brother Cowley has risen to high rank in his profession, that of attorney and jurist, in his state. He stands among the best writers in a state that is renowned for the eminence of its authors; for scholarly attainments, and for thorough knowledge of the classics, he is esteemed as the peer of the brightest.

The *Vox Populi*, whose editor has often spoken with fine felicity on Pythian occasions, says: "The Knights of Pythias, and all persons of scholarly tastes, owe a debt of gratitude to Charles Cowley, LL. D., of Lowell, for his exhaustive researches among the literary remains of Grecian and Roman civilization, which have enabled him to present to them all the Greek and Latin versions of the beautiful story of Damon and Pythias which have survived the ravages of time."

The well-known author, Rev. Elias Nason, D. D., says: "As Edward Everett traced to its origin the rabbinical story of Abraham and the strangers, so has Judge Cowley quite as well explored to its remotest sources the classical story of these pattern friends."

In Pythian matters he has taken a very deep interest, and is now one of the Past Grand Chancellors of Massachusetts, honored, respected, and loved by all who know him.

And now we give what he has to say of the ancient versions of the story of Damon and Pythias:

Knights of Pythias, and all persons of scholarly tastes, are presumably interested to know the results which the researches of many years have yielded, touching the story of Damon and Pythias. Five versions of this beautiful story are extant, which were written within a thousand years after the episode which they commemorate; three of these are found among the remains of ancient Greek literature, and two among the remains of the ancient Latin literature. Some of them have been repeatedly published in English translations; others of them have never appeared in our language before.

There were, unquestionably, earlier writers whose works have perished, by whom this story was handed down. There was certainly one writer, and very probably another, who lived when this episode occurred, and whose works, though lost to us, were extant for ages, and are known to have been read by some of the later authors whose versions are herewith presented.

Aristoxenus, the earliest writer who is known to have recorded this story, lived at Corinth, in the fourth century before Christ, contemporaneously with Damon and Pythias, and obtained his information directly from Dionysius the Younger, who, after his second expulsion from Syracuse, lived at Corinth, supporting himself by teaching. Philistus, the historian of Syracuse, probably mentioned this episode in his history. He, like Aristoxenus, was a contemporary of Dionysius, and the pair of pattern friends; but his writings, like those of Aristoxenus, have been lost for a thousand years.

The oldest version now extant is that of Cicero, who lived about three hundred years after Damon and Pythias, during the first century before Christ. His version is as follows:

"Damon and Pythias, two of the followers of Pythagoras, were so closely attached to each other that when Dionysius, the tyrant, ordered one of them to be put to death on a certain day, and the party condemned begged for a respite of a few days, so that he might go home to attend to his own before he should die, the other voluntarily became his substitute, to die in his place if he did not appear. At the time appointed the condemned returned to meet his fate. Thereupon the tyrant was so much amazed at their extraordinary fidelity that he sought to be admitted as a third in their friendship."—*Cicero, De Officiis, Book III., Chap.* 10.

On another occasion, referring to this episode by way of illustration, Cicero writes substantially as follows:

" How low was the estimate which Dionysius put upon those friendships which he feared would fail, he shows by what he says of those two disciples of Pythagoras, Damon and Pythias; for, when he had accepted one of them as a substitute for the other who was doomed to die, and when the other, to redeem his surety's life, had promptly returned at the hour appointed for his execution, Dionysius said to them, ' Would that I could be enrolled as your third friend.' How unhappy was Dionysius' lot, to be thus deprived of the communion of friends, the social intercourse and familiar converse of daily life."—*Cicero, Tusculan Disputations, Book V., Chap.* 22.

The second oldest version now extant is that of Diodorus Siculus, who wrote his history a little after the time of Cicero and a little before the time of Christ, and who, like Cicero, probably read the works of Aristoxenus, and certainly read the works of Philistus. His version of this Damo-Pythian episode is as follows:

"Phintias, a certain Pythagorean, having conspired against the tyrant, and being about to suffer the penalty, besought from Dionysius previous opportunity to arrange his private affairs as he desired, and he said that he would give one of his friends as surety for himself. As the despot wondered whether there was such a friend, who would put himself in the bastile in his stead, Phintias called a certain one of his companions, Damon by name, a Pythagorean philosopher, who, nothing doubting, immediately became substitute for Phintias. Thereupon some commended the extravagant regard existing between these friends, while others, indeed, condemned the rashness and folly of the substitute.

"Now, at the appointed time, all the people assembled, eager to see whether he who had made this recognizance would keep his pledge. Indeed, the hour was already drawing to a close, and all had given up Damon in despair, when Phintias, having accomplished his purpose, came running at full speed, at the turn of the critical moment, just as Damon was being led away to execution. At this manifestation of most remarkable friendship, Dionysius revoked the sentence, pardoned all concerned, and called on the men, Damon and Phintias, to receive himself as a third into their friendship."—*Diodorus, Book X., Chap.* 4.

This history, which filled forty books and embodied the labor of thirty years, was written in Greek, and much of it has been lost.

The third oldest version now extant is that of Valerius Maximus, who lived contemporaneously with Diodorus, and wrote very soon after him. He wrote in Latin, as did Cicero; though, like Cicero, he was familiar with the Greek. His account is this:

"Damon and Pythias, having been initiated into the sacred

rites of the Pythagorean society, were united together by such strong friendship, that when Dionysius, the Syracusan, purposed to kill one of them, and he had obtained from him a respite, by which, before he should die, he might return home and arrange his affairs, the other did not hesitate to become surety for his return to the tyrant. He who was free from danger of death, in this way submitted his neck to the sword; he who was allowed to live in security risked his head for his friend. Thereupon all, and especially Dionysius, watched the result of this new and uncertain affair. When the appointed day approached, and he did not return, every one condemned the rash surety for his folly; but he declared that for himself he did not at all doubt the constancy of his friend. However, at this moment, even at the hour determined by Dionysius, he who had received the respite returned.

"The tyrant, admiring the disposition of both, remitted the punishment of the friend; and, moreover, he requested that they would receive him into their society of friendship as the third member of the brotherhood, as the greatest kindness and honor. Such friendship indeed begets contempt for death, is able to break the charm of life, to make the savage gentle, to repay punishment with kindness and to transform hatred into love. It merits almost as much reverence as the sacred rites of the immortal gods; for while these preserve public safety, that conserves private good; and as sacred temples are the places of religious rites, so the faithful hearts of such men are like temples filled by a special divine influence."—*Valerius Maximus, Liber IV., Chap. 7, Ext.* 1.

The fourth oldest version now extant is that of Porphyry, who flourished during the latter part of the third century after Christ, and who avowedly follows the version of Aristoxenus, as quoted by Nicomachus, a Pythagorean, of Gerasa, who wrote during the reign of the Emperor Tiberius. Porphyry's version is in Greek, and no English translation of it has ever before been published. It is as follows:

"Pity and tears, and all such, these men, Damon and Phintias [or Pythias], excite; this certainly is admitted. Now this is the account, as well of the flattery and of the entreaty and of the prayer, as of all such as these. When, on a certain occasion, some having said that when the Pythagoreans were apprehended, they did not stand to their pledge to one another, Dionysius, wishing to make trial of them, thus arranged : Phintias was seized and brought before the tyrant; then accused that he had conspired against him; indeed, he was convicted of this, and it was determined to put him to death. Then he [Phintias] spake, that since it had thus happened to him, at least the rest of the day should be given to him in order that he might arrange his own private affairs, and also those of Damon, who was a companion and copartner with himself, and he, being the elder, much of what concerned the management of their business was referred to him. When asked that a substitute be furnished, he offered Damon; and Dionysius, having consented to this, sent for Damon, who, having heard what had happened, became surety, and remained until Phintias should return. Then, indeed, Dionysius was astonished at these results. But they who from the beginning had prosecuted the trial jeered Damon as having been entrapped. Yet, when it was about the setting of the sun, Phintias came back to be put to death. At this all were astonished. Then Dionysius, having embraced and kissed the friends, requested them to receive him as a third into their friendship; but, although he very earnestly besought it, they would by no means agree to such request. This much, indeed, Aristoxenus declared that he had heard from Dionysius himself [meaning Dionysius the Younger]."—*Porphyry, "Life of Pythagoras."*

Porphyry adds that Hippobotus and Neanthus relate this story of Mylius and Timychia; but the story related of Mylius and Timychia is essentially different from this.

The fifth oldest version now extant is that of Iamblichus, a pupil of Porphyry, who also wrote a life of Pythagoras in Greek, containing many matters from preceding authors whose works are lost. Imablichus lived as late as the reign of Julian the Apostate, and he derives his version avowedly directly from Aristoxenus; it is as follows :

" When Dionysius, having been expelled from his tyranny, came to Corinth, he often entertained us with the particulars touching the Pythagoreans, Phintias and Damon, and the circumstances under which one became surety for the other in a case of death. He said that some of those who were familiar with him frequently misrepresented the Pythagoreans, defaming and reviling them, stigmatizing them as impostors, and saying that their temperance, their gravity, and their confidence in one another were assumed, and that this would become apparent if any one should place them in distress or surround them with disaster. Others denied this, and contention arising on the subject, recourse was had to artifice.

"One of the prosecutors accused Phintias to his face of having conspired with others against the life of Dionysius, and this was testified to by those present, and was made to appear exceedingly probable. Phintias was astonished at the accusation. But when Dionysius declared, unequivocally, that he had carefully investigated the affair, and that Phintias should die, Phintias replied, that since it had befallen him to be thus accused, he desired that at least the rest of the day might be allowed to him, so that he might arrange his own affairs, and also those of Damon; for these men collected the vintage from all around into wine-cellars, and disposed of it in common; and Phintias, being the elder, had assumed for the most part the management of their domestic concerns. He therefore requested the tyrant to allow him to depart for this purpose, and named Damon as his surety. Dionysius was surprised at this request, and asked whether there was such a man who would risk death by becoming surety for another. So Phintias requested him to send for Damon, who, on hearing what had taken place, said he would become sponsor for Phintias, and that he would remain there till Phintias returned. Dionysius was deeply impressed by these results; but those who introduced the experiment derided Damon as having been left in the lurch, and mocking him, said that he would be devoted as a stag to sacrifice. But when it was already about sundown, Phintias came back to be put to death, at which all that were present were astonished and overpowered. Wherefore, Dionysius, having embraced and kissed the friends, requested that they would receive him as a third into their friendship; but they would by no means consent to such a thing, although he earnestly besought it. Now, indeed, Aristoxenus relates these things as having learned them from Dionysius himself."—*Iamblichus, Life of Pythagoras,* § 223.

In connection with the versions of these writers, it is proper to add that Plutarch, who flourished in the first century of our era, refers to Damon and Pythias in his "Morals." The reference is in his tract "On the Folly of Seeking Many Friends," where he asks, "What report does the record of antiquity make concerning true friends? They are always recorded in pairs: as Theseus and Pirithous, Achilles and Patroclus, Orestes and Pylades, Phintias and Damon, Epaminondas and Pelopidas. Friendship is a creature sociable, including one's self and a companion; showing that two is the adequate and complete measure of friendship."—*Goodwin's Plutarch's Morals, Vol. I., p.* 465.

It will be observed that certain alterations and additions have been made to this story, as successive versions of it have appeared. The translators of the Greek and Latin versions have also embellished (or rather disfigured) it with other additions derived from their own imagination.

Thus, Dr. Cockman, in his translation of Cicero's "Offices," represents Phintias as desiring time "wherein he might provide for his children," but the original text, "*commendandorum suorum causa postulavisset,*" scarcely warrants the inference that Phintias ever had a wife or children; and, perhaps, the fact, mentioned by Iamblichus, that Damon and Pythias carried on business as copartners, may warrant the inference that they were bachelors.

Again, Thomas Taylor, the new Platonist, in his translation of Iamblichus' version of this Damo-Pythian episode, says that Damon and Pythias "lived together and had all things in common." But the Greek text of Iamblichus contains nothing which indicates that they "had all things in common." They were not socialists, although, with the help of their slaves, they carried on business as wine merchants, and perhaps kept bachelor's hall together.

Dramatists and other poets, like Edwards, Chettle, Barnes, Banim, Lessing, Schiller, and Bates, and historical romance writers like Soave, may represent one of these immortal friends as a senator, the other as a knight, and may surround them with fathers, mothers, brothers, sons, sisters, sweethearts, wives, and daughters. Poetic license permits this. But with history it is not so. While the historian is bound to tell all that he knows, he is equally bound not to tell any more than he knows; and the foregoing fragments contain all that we know of this pair of pattern friends. "The rest is silence."

Not alone as a Latin or Greek scholar, but in the study of the modern languages, and the study and translation of modern authors, does Judge Cowley take equally high rank. Following his translation of the accounts given by the Greek and Roman authors, we give herewith his translation of the famous dialogue, written in French by the Most Rev. Francis Fenelon, Archbishop of Cambray. This dialogue is based on the account of Valerius Maximus.

DIALOGUE BETWEEN DIONYSIUS, DAMON, AND PYTHIAS.

DIONYSIUS. *Amazing!* What do I see? Pythias—returned! It is, indeed, Pythias. I never thought it possible. After all, he has come back to die, to redeem his friend.

PYTHIAS. Yes, it is Pythias. I left my dungeon to pay my vows to Heaven, to settle my affairs, and bid my family a last adieu; and now I am satisfied, and can die in peace.

DIONYSIUS. But why have you returned? Have you no love of life or dread of death? Why, man, you are mad, to throw away your life in this way.

PYTHIAS. I have come back to die, though I have done nothing to deserve it. But my honor forbids me to break my word, or to allow my friend to die in my place.

DIONYSIUS. What, then, do you love Damon better than yourself?

PYTHIAS. No; but I love him as myself; and I know that I ought to die rather than Damon; for it was I that was adjudged to death. It would be most unjust that Damon should perish to save me from the scaffold which has been erected, not for him, but for me.

DIONYSIUS. But you think it is as unjust to put you to death as it is to put Damon to death.

PYTHIAS. Very true; we are both perfectly innocent; and the death of one of us is as unjust as the death of the other.

DIONYSIUS. Then why is it more unjust to put Damon to death than yourself?

PYTHIAS.   It is as unjust that I should suffer as that Damon should suffer; yet it would be most cruel and unjust in me to permit Damon to suffer the penalty which was imposed, though most unjustly, for my act alone.

DIONYSIUS.   You mean to say, then, that you have come back on the day assigned for your execution with no other motive than this fastidious honor, and solely for the purpose of saving Damon's life by sacrificing your own!

PYTHIAS.   I have come back, so far as you are concerned, to suffer an unjust and cruel penalty, too common under such governments as yours; but as to Damon, I am come merely to perform my duty, by rescuing him from the peril which his own generosity assumed by becoming surety for my return.

DIONYSIUS.   And now, Damon, I will hear you.   Had you no fear that Pythias would fail to return,—and that you, as his surety, would be executed in his stead?

DAMON.   O, I never had a doubt that Pythias would come back.   I know the integrity and fidelity of the man; and I knew he would be far more anxious to keep faith with me than to save his own life.   For myself, I wish his family and friends had kept him at home.   If his life had thus been preserved he would have lived as a benefactor, not only to his own family, but to Syracuse, to Sicily, and to the world.   Under such circumstances I should have died without regret.

DIONYSIUS.   Is life then a burden to you, that you are so ready to throw it away?

DAMON.   This world—this kingdom of Sicily—has no charm for me—where my life, my liberty, and my property can be taken from me at any moment, at the word or nod of a tyrant.

DIONYSIUS.   Very well, then.   You shall see Pythias no more.   I will order you to immediate execution.

PYTHIAS.   Pardon the feelings of a man who has sympathy for his dying friend.   Remember, it was I whom you doomed to death; and here I have come to suffer that death in order that I might redeem my friend.   Pray, do not deny me this one consolation in my last hour.

DIONYSIUS.   But men who despise death, and set my government at defiance, are not to be endured in Syracuse.

DAMON. Cannot virtue be endured in Syracuse? Is it nothing that a man is so faithful to his friendships that he will pledge his own life to redeem his friend?

DIONYSIUS. Friendship is well enough in its place; but what I cannot endure is that proud, disdainful virtue, which holds life in contempt, which has no dread of death, and for which wealth and pleasure has no charm.

DAMON. And yet you see that virtue which you despise is not insensible to the dictates of Honor, Justice, and Friendship.

DIONYSIUS. Oh, I see it is useless to parley with such men. Guards, take Pythias to the scaffold. Let us see whether Damon will respect my authority.

DAMON. Pardon a single word. Pythias, by coming back and submitting himself to your displeasure, has merited your favor, and deserves to live; while I have excited your indignation by resigning myself to your power, in order to save him. Pray, let one life atone for both; be content with one sacrifice, and let me be put to death.

PYTHIAS. Hold, Dionysius! Remember, it was Pythias alone who offended you. Damon could not—

DIONYSIUS. Gracious Heavens! What do I see and hear? Where am I, and what am I? Utterly wretched and miserable, and so I deserve to be. I have known nothing of true virtue till now. I have passed my life without love. I have had wealth, office, honor, power; but these cannot buy friendship; —they can never win love. For thirty years I have swayed Sicily and Syracuse. I have had a host of sycophants, but I have never had a single friend, who deserved that name. And here, these two men, in private life, love one another, trust one another, confide in one another, are thoroughly happy in one another, and either of them would be glad to die to save the other.

PYTHIAS. How could you, Dionysius, who have never loved any one yourself, expect to win friends? Had you yourself loved or respected other men, you would thereby have won their love and respect in return. But you loathe and dread all mankind, and they, as a natural consequence, loathe and dread you.

DIONYSIUS.. Damon — Pythias — your attachment to each other is wonderful. It is a revelation to me which I would not forget. Will you—can you—admit me as a third member in a union that is so perfect? I freely give you your lives; and I will open to both of you the road to wealth and fame.

DAMON. We have no wish for riches. The philosopher, whose disciples we are, has taught us a higher code of ethics than you would care to accept. The virtue which he inculcates is a constant endeavor to represent everywhere on earth the beauty, the unity, and the harmony which is everywhere displayed in the order of the universe. How could you, who have for fifty years given free play to every passion, now acquire that mastery of all your passions which Pythagoras insists on as indispensable in his disciples? We should be glad of your friendship; but we could not accept it without these qualifications. One word more, Dionysius, before we quit your presence. You would have friends; but, except upon these conditions, the desire is a vain longing. You have—and while in power you can always have—slavish sycophants and vile flatterers; but to be beloved and esteemed by free and generous souls, you must yourself learn to live as they live, and acquire their virtues.

CHAPTER IV.

THE POETIC DAMON AND PYTHIAS.

WORLD at large knows Damon and Pythias through the story as presented by the young Irish author, dramatist and poet, John Banim. It might be said of this author that in his hands and those of Shiel, who aided him, the names and fame of the two friends, Damon and Pythias, were resurrected and crowned with greater glory than that which adorned the historic pair in the days of Dionysius, the tyrant.

The drama was first produced on the 28th of May, 1821, at the Covent Garden Theatre. The cast was made up from the very best actors of that time, and the success of the drama was unprecedented. The story, as told by Valerius Maximus, has not been materially altered in so far as the friendship and self-sacrificing devotion of Damon and Pythias for one another is concerned. The two characters have, however, in the hands of the poet, changed places, so that Pythias has become the hostage instead of Damon. As before stated, the history of the Knights of Pythias would not be complete without this drama, any more than the description of a mighty river without pointing out the spring from which it took its rise. This drama was the spring from which has come our great Pythian river that to-day is bearing such a vast flotilla through life's storms and billows into the

DAMON AND PYTHIAS.

great harbor of rest, and it was from this version of the lives of these two friends that the Founder of the Order drew his inspiration. This drama, in its lesson of devotion and friendship, is the exponent of Pythian doctrine as taught by our Order, and it will so stand for all time to come.

So, as a part of our history, as a part of the literature, of the world that is now the property of the Order of Knights of Pythias, we publish here the

DRAMA OF DAMON AND PYTHIAS.

ACT I.

SCENE I.—*A street in Syracuse.*

DIONYSIUS *and* PROCLES *discovered, as expecting tidings.*

Dion. Ere this the senate should have closed its councils,
And chosen the new year's president. I pant
To know their meeting's issue.
    Proc. Good my lord,
There's but light doubt a great majority
Of easy-purchased voices will be found
For your fast friend, Philistius.
    Dion. On his choice
Hangs the long chain of complicated purpose
Has ta'en such time in linking. Plague upon
The law, that from the senate-house excludes
All soldiers, like ourselves, or we should soon
Outvote all difficulty!
Ha! methinks the assembly hath dissolved.
By Jupiter!
Philistius' self doth hasten to us here,
And with him Damocles! How now, my friend?

Enter PHILISTIUS *and* DAMOCLES.

Art thou the president?
    Phil. I am, my lord.
Chosen by a large majority to take

The honorable office in the which
I may, at least, requite the benefits
Which you have heaped upon me.
    Dam. Yes, my lord,
We have at last attained the 'vantage ground,
Whence your broad view may take a boundless prospect.
    Dion. 'Tis a bold step upon the mountain-path,
Wherein I have been toiling.   I no longer
Doubt of the senate's inclination.
[*To Procles.*] What say the soldiers?   Thou hast hinted to them
That we confided to thee?
    Proc. Yes, my lord;
And they are ready for it.
    Dion. Go thou hence,
And speak to them again; disperse more gold;
'Twill give a relish to thine eloquence;
And, hark ye, lead them this way; I shall here
Await thy coming.   Ha! behold in air,
Where a majestic eagle floats above
The northern turrets of the citadel;
And, as the sun breaks through yon rifted cloud,
His plumage shines, embathed in burning gold,
And sets off his regality in heaven!
Thou knowest how readily the multitude
Are won by such bright augury—make use
Of divination—haste thee!   [*Exit Procles.*
Philistius, give me your hand.   I thank you.
Things look in smiles upon me.   It was otherwise
But a year since, when I impeached the magistrates
For treasonable dealing with the foe,
And the senate hurled me from my topmost height
Of popularity.
    Dam. Degraded you
From power and office.
    Dion. Ay! at the appeal
Of that stale pedant, the Pythagorean,
Who hangs out his austerity for sale,
In frowns, closed lips, and pithy sentences.
    Dam. Thou speakest of Damon?

Dion. Ay, mine enemy,
The patriot and philosophic knave,
Who hath been busy with my purposes,
And one day shall not smile at it.   He came
Into the senate-house, with a fierce crew
Of his associates in philosophy,
Silent and frowning, at his back; he railed,
And had his triumph.—Times have altered since;
And, to the mould and fashion of my will,
Shall yet take stranger shape, when, Damocles,
These long-trained law-givers, these austere sages,
Shall find I can remember.

"*Dam.* Let them feel it.

"*Dion.* In all that biting bitterness of heart
"Which clings, and gnaws, by inches, to its object,
"More keen, because a first essay hath failed,
"In shame and suffering, failed, thus have I sped
"My work, in silence, on.   It did become
"A thought inwoven with my inmost being."

Dam. The steps
Which since most visibly you have ascended,
Must have required much effort?

Dion. Yes! to have flung
Into the shade of public disrepute,
The very men whose voices were most loud
In working out my ruin; after that,
To gain the army's suffrage;—to be chosen
Its head and general, that was another;
To have won that very senate—

Phil. Yet pause, my lord:
Howe'er complying you have hitherto
Found that assembly, and though most of them
Are plunged into your debt, beyond all means
Of their redemption, yet may there be still
Some sudden reluctation to the last
And mightiest of all hopes.

Dion. The garrison
Is not a bad ally, methinks?

Phil. The war
Hath ta'en the flower of all the troops from Syracuse,
And Damon heading the vile populace—
        Dion. I came from Agrigentum to entreat
Arms, corn, and money from the senators,
While I myself have purposely delayed
The granting them; meantime, the city is filled
With many thousands of my followers.
        Phil. But are they not unweaponed?
        Dion. This city of Syracuse—
It hath a citadel?
        Phil. True, sir; it hath.
        Dion. And therein, as I deem, its national stock
Of corn, and arms, and gold is treasured?
        Phil. True.
        Dion. The citadel is not impregnable;
And when it is manned and ordered to my will,
What of these frothy speech-makers?   [*Shouts are heard.*
        Phil. My Lord,
The soldiers shout for you.
        Dion. Procles, I see,
Is at his work.—Good Damocles, Philistius,
As you are senators, retire you hence;
It were not meet that you should look to have been
Parties to any act which afterwards
May grow into discussion.—And, Philistius,
One effort more among our city friends:
I will forewarn thee of the time to call
The senators together.—Yet, I mean not
Exclusively to trust them, good Philistius;—
Sure means, sure ends.—I'll have a friend or two
Within my call, to help them.—If their councils
Become too knotty for unravelling,
A sharp sword may be useful.—Fare you well.
                        [*Exeunt Philistius and Damocles.*
    [*Voices without.*] Ay, to the citadel!—The citadel!

            Enter PROCLES *and* SOLDIERS.

    Dion. Who talks of moving to the citadel?

Proc. It is himself—huzza!

All. Huzza! our general!

Dion. Good friends, I thank ye.   Procles, art thou here?
Hast thou distributed to these much-wronged men
The trifling bounty which I charged thee with?

Proc. They have it, noble general.

Dion. My friends,
'Twas a poor offering, and beneath your taking;
But, as yourselves do know, my private purse
Is light as that of any other veteran   ,
Within the walls of Syracuse.   Speak, Procles;—
Who talks of moving to the citadel?

Proc. We, Dionysius, we.   Yes, these brave spirits;
Indignant at the senate's heedlessness
Of you, and them, and of the general honor.

Dion. Give me not cause, my friends, to deem myself
Dishonored and endangered in your love;
For, as I am a soldier and a man,
Could I believe that any other thought
Engaged you to possess the citadel,
Save your anxiety for the soldier's weal,
And the state's safety, I would raise my hand
In supplication 'gainst your enterprise;—
But, as the time now urges, and cries out
For sudden muster and organization
Of the brave thousands who but wait for swords
To join your ranks, and rush with you to glory;—
And yet the senate—

Proc. Speak not of the senate:
We do renounce its service, and despise it.

Dion. It was my thought to say, if they object,
We may submit it as a needful step;
Claiming allowance in the exigency
Of the occasion.

Proc. They shall not control it.
We seek not for their judgment of our act.
On, general, on!

Dion. When did ye call,
That I replied not with my word and deed,

My heart and hand?   Even as you say it, on!
On, fellow-soldiers, to the citadel!   [*Draws his sword.*
And let your swords be out, more in the show
Of what ye are, soldiers and fighting men,
Than with a harmful purpose.   Let us on!
     All. On to the citadel!—the citadel!
                    [*Exeunt with cries, and brandishing their swords.*

Enter DAMON.

Damon. Philistius, then, is president at last,
And Dionysius has o'erswayed it?   Well,
It is what I expected.   There is now
No public virtue left in Syracuse.
What should be hoped from a degenerate,
Corrupted, and voluptuous populace,
When highly-born and meanly-minded nobles
Would barter freedom for a great man's feast,
And sell their country for a smile?   The stream
With a more sure eternal tendency
Seeks not the ocean, than a sensual race
Their own devouring slavery.   I am sick,
At my immost heart, of everything I see
And hear!   Oh, Syracuse, I am, at last,
Forced to despair of thee!   And yet thou art
My land of birth—thou art my country still;
And, like an unkind mother, thou hast left
The claims of holiest nature in my heart,
And I must sorrow for, not hate thee!   [*Shouts are heard.*
What shouts are these?   'Tis from the citadel.
The uproar is descending.

Enter LUCULLUS.

Speak, Lucullus!
What has befallen?
     Luc. Have you not heard the news?
     Damon. What news?
     Luc. As through the streets I passed, the people
Said that the citadel was in the hands
Of Dionysius.

Damon. The citadel
In Dionysius' hands?   What dost thou tell me?
How—wherefore—when ?   In Dionysius' hands—
The traitor Dionysius?—Speak, Lucullus,
And quickly!
    Luc. It was said, that by rude force,
Heading a troop of soldiers, he had ta'en
Possession of the citadel, and seized
The arms and treasure in't.   [*Exit Lucullus.*
    Damon. I am thunder-stricken!
The citadel assaulted, and the armory
In that fierce soldier's power! [*Shouts are heard.*] Again!   By all
The gods on high Olympus, I behold
His standard waving o'er it—and they come,
His most notorious satellites, high heaped
With arms and plunder!   Parricidal slaves!
What have ye done?   [*Shouts are heard.*

Enter PROCLES, OFFICERS, *and* SOLDIERS.

    Proc. and Sol. For Dionysius!   Ho!
For Dionysius!
    Damon. Silence! obstreperous traitors!
Your throats offend the quiet of the city;
And thou, who standest foremost of these knaves,
Stand back, and answer me—a senator,
What have you done?
    Proc. But that I know 'twill gall thee,
Thou poor and talking pedant of the school
Of dull Pythagoras, I'd let thee make
Conjecture from thy senses; but, in hope
'Twill stir your solemn anger, learn from me
We have ta'en possession of the citadel,
And—
    Damon. Patience, ye good gods! a moment's patience,
That these too ready hands may not enforce
The desperate precept of my rising heart—
Thou most contemptible and meanest tool
That ever tyrant used!

Proc. Do you hear him, soldiers?
First, for thy coward railings at myself,
And since thou hast called our Dionysius tyrant,
Here, in the open streets of Syracuse,
I brand thee for a liar and a traitor.
   Damon. Audacious slave!
   Proc. Upon him, soldiers!
Hew him to pieces!
   Soldiers. On him!   [*They advance, shouting.*

     Enter PYTHIAS, *as they rush upon Damon.*

   Pyth. Back, on your lives!
Cowards, damned, treacherous cowards, back, I say!
Do you know me? Look upon me: do you know
This honest sword I brandish? You have seen it
Among the ranks of Carthage; would you now
Taste its shrewd coldness in your quaking selves?
             [*Officers and Soldiers advance.*
Back! back! I say. He hath his armor on—
I am his sword, shield, helm; I but enclose
Myself, and my own heart, and heart's blood, when
I stand before him thus.
   Damon. Falsehearted cravens!
We are but two—my Pythias, my halved heart!—
My Pythias, and myself! but dare come on,
Ye hirelings of a tyrant! dare advance
A foot, or raise an arm, or bend a brow,
And ye shall learn what two such arms can do
Amongst a thousand of ye.   [*Soldiers advance.*
   Pyth. Off!
Off, villians, off!—Each for the other thus,
And in that other, for his dearer self!
Why, Procles, art thou not ashamed—for I
Have seen thee do good work in battle time—
Art not ashamed, here on a single man
To rush in coward numbers? Fie upon thee!
I took thee for a soldier.

PYTHIAS DEFENDING DAMON.

Proc. For thy sake,
Who art a warrior like ourselves, we spare him.
'Twas a good star of his that led thee hither
From Agrigentum, to lift up thine arm
In the defence of that long robe of peace
Wherein he wraps his stern philosophy.
Come, teach him better manners.   Soldiers, on !
Let us to Dionysius.

          [*Exeunt Procles, Officers, and Soldiers, shouting.*

   Pyth. Art thou safe
From these infuriate stabbers ?

   Damon. Thanks to thee,
I am safe, my gallant soldier, and fast friend :
My better genius sent thee to my side,
When I did think thee far from Syracuse.

   Pyth. I have won leave to spend some interval
From the fierce war, and come to Syracuse
With purpose to espouse the fair Calanthe.—
The gods have led me hither, since I come
In time to rescue thee.
How grew this rude broil up ?

   Damon. Things go on here
Most execrably, Pythias.   But you are come
To be a husband, are you not ?

   Pyth. To-morrow
I call my soft Calanthe wife.

   Damon. Then, Pythias,
I will not shade the prospect of your joys
With any griefs of mine.   I cry you mercy—
These are experiments too over nice
For one that has a mistress, and would wed her
With an uncut throat.   I have oft wished, myself,
That to the blest retreats of private life
My lot had been awarded; every hour
Makes one more sick and weary with the sense
Of this same hopeless service of a state,
Where there is not enough of virtue left
To feed the flarings of our liberty.

But, my soldier,
I will not make thee a participant
In my most sad forebodings.—Pythias,
I say 'twere better to be the Persian's slave,
And let him tread upon thee, when he would
Ascend his horse's back, than—yet, not so;
I am too much galled and fretted to pronounce
A sober judgment, and the very mask
Of freedom is yet better than the bold,
Uncovered front of tyranny.—Farewell!

   Pyth. Nay, I must follow thee, and find the cause
That so perturbs thy spirit.

   Damon. How, sir! You have
A mistress here in Syracuse, and, look,
Herself comes forth to meet you.

   Pyth. Where? Calanthe!
Nay, I behold her not—you mock me, Damon.

   Damon. [*Pointing in a different direction.*]
Look this way, sir.

   Pyth. It is herself, indeed,
My own, my fond, betrothéd one.   [*Runs to meet her.*

Enter CALANTHE.

   Cal. My dear,
But most neglecting Pythias!

   Pyth. By the birth
Of Venus, when she rose out of the sea,
And with her smile did fill the Grecian isles
With everlasting verdure, she was not,
Fresh from the soft creation of the wave,
More beautiful than thou!

   Cal. Thou fondly thinkest
To hide thy false oblivion of the maid
That, with a panting heart, awaited thee.
Now, Pythias, I do take it most unkind,
That thou to friendship hast made sacrifice
Of the first moment of thy coming here.

   Pyth. Nay, chide me not, for I was speeding to thee.

Cal. Soon as I heard thou wert in Syracuse
I ran at once to hail thee with a smile,
Although my mother would have staid me.

[*Pythias kisses her hand.*

Damon. [*Lost in thought.*] Yes,
My wife and child—
They must at least be safe.

Pyth. And how, Calanthe,
Fares thy dear mother?

Cal. Happy in the thought,
If she must needs (as she must) part with me,
It is at least to *thee.*

Pyth. And my poor father?

Cal. Time has almost shut up his faculties;
And he can scarce distinguish any voice
That is addressed to him.   The day is passed
Upon his couch; at evening, in a chair,
He is carried to the terrace walk before
The threshold of his mansion, where the wind,
Fresh from the sea, plays with his locks of gray,
'Til, pleased at last, he smiles.   That gentle smile,
As 'tis the first denotement of a thought
In speechless infancy, 'tis the last sign
Of the expiring mind.

Pyth. My soft Calanthe
Must be a tender on infirmity
Before her time.   But where's my silent friend?

Damon. [*Aside, and lost in thought.*] One brave blow
And it were done!   By all the gods, one blow
And Syracuse were free!

Pyth. [*Touching him on the shoulder.*] Why, Damon, what's
     the matter?

Damon. Pythias, is't you?
[*To Calanthe.*] I cry you mercy, fair one!   Pythias,
You are to be married.   Haste thee, Pythias,—
Love, and fight on.   Thine arm to Mars, thy heart
Give to his paramour.—Take thou no care
Of the politician's study—'twill turn pale

Thy face, make thee grow sick at nature's loveliness,
And find in her pure beauty but one blank
Of dismal, colorless sterility.
Calanthe, look to it: let him not play
The statesman's sorry part.
    Pyth. Damon, you let
The commonwealth o'erfret you.   I was about
To pray you to our wedding.
    Damon. I intended,
Unbidden, to be there.
    Pyth. From friendship's eyes
I'll win addition to my happiness.
Calanthe, come—I should be half in fear,
To seem thus loving of thee. in the sight
Of this philosopher.
    Cal. Nay, he pretends
To be by half more rugged and more wise,
Than he hath any right to: I have seen him,
(Have I not, Damon?) looking at his wife,
When he imagined none was there to mark
The proud Pythagorean, with an eye
Filled up with tenderness:—and his young boy, too,
That seems Aurora's child, with his fine face,
Stirred his stern visage to complacency.
Come, come, we'll be revenged upon you both:
I swear, his wife and I will be accounted
Your rivals in the godlike quality
Your lordly sex would arrogate its own
Peculiar privilege, and show the world
Th' unseen, and yet unrumored prodigy—
The friendship of a woman.   [*Exeunt Calanthe and Pythias.*

Enter LUCULLUS.

Damon. Hark thee, Lucullus:
My wife and child must instantly depart
From Syracuse;—you must attend them hence,
Unto my villa, on the mountain side.
    Luc. Alas, my lord!
    Damon. Why dost thou droop?

Luc. My lord,
I was your slave; you gave me liberty;
And when I see you perilled—
Damon. Nay, Lucullus,
Where is the warrant for thy fear?
Luc. I read
You are engaged in some dread enterprise,
Else you would not deny them to your sight:
You fear the leaning ruin may fall down
Upon their dearer heads.
Damon. I charge you, sir,
No prying into my purposes.—Take care
You speak not to my wife of anything
May stir her apprehensions—see, she comes—
Beware—thy looks betray thee.   [*Lucullus retires.*

Enter HERMION.

Her. Art thou safe,
Damon, art safe?
Damon. You are not a widow yet.
Her. For shame to talk of such a thing.   I have heard
Of thy rude quarrelling with that same fierce
And overbearing soldier.   But thou art safe.—
Proud men! how reckless of the faithful hearts
That dote on you—that hang their weakness on ye!
How reckless of us in your bustling hours
Of occupation and despatch ye are!
Ah, then you think not of the pining mate,
Left in her solitude, with naught to do
But weep for your return, and chide the gods
That make your minds so stern and enterprising.
Damon. Hermion, I think the city's fulsome air
Likes not our boy:—the color in his cheek
Hath lost its rich and healthful purity.
Her. Nay, you are wrong there;—'tis like a young peach;
Or yet *more* fresh and blooming.
Damon. Hermion,
I have resolved that you and he shall go
Unto my villa, near to Syracuse.
Her. But you will come with us?

Damon. Hermion, you know
My occupation forbids that wish.
   Luc. [*Advancing.*] My lord—
   Damon. Forbear, sir —[*Lucullus retires*]—yet I cannot go—
I mean, I cannot go immediately—
The state affairs lay hold upon me.   You
Must hence before me thither.
   Her. Damon—
   ·*Damon.* Come,
Look not thus sadly.
   Her. I have learned too well
The usage of obedience, to inquire
Into your purposes.
   Damon. Hermion, I'll take
Occasion oft to visit you—to-morrow—
If possible, to-morrow.
   Her. Will you so ?
Nay, will you truly promise it ?
   Damon. I do.—
Hermion, you must be sudden ; you must despatch.
Come—but I'll see my boy before you go.
Hermion, he is our only one.   That child
Is made of thy own heart and mine.   I charge thee,
Have thou a care, in all vicissitudes
Of private or of public incident,
To form in him what will out-top the height
Of the best laurel-tree in all the groves
Of the Academy—an honest man.   [*Exeunt.*

ACT II.

Scene I.—*A Chamber in Arria's House.*

Enter Pythias *and* Calanthe.

Pyth. So, my Calanthe, you would waste the moon
Of Hymen in this lonely spot ?
   Cal. In sooth,
I would, for 'tis the fairest place in Sicily :

A dell, made of green beauty; with its shrubs
Of aromatic sweetness growing up
The rugged mountain's sides, as cunningly
As the nice structure of a little nest,
Built by two loving nightingales. "The wind
"That comes there, full of rudeness from the sea,
"Is lulled into a balmy breath of peace
"The moment that it enters; and 'tis said
"By our Sicilian shepherds, that their songs
"Have in this place a wilder melody.
"The mountains all about it are the haunts
"Of many a fine romantic memory!
"High towers old Ætna, with his feet deep clad
"In the green sandals of the freshful spring;
"His sides arrayed in winter, and his front
"Shooting aloft the everlasting flame.
"On the right hand is the great cave, in which
"Huge Polyphemus dwelt, between whose vast
"Colossal limbs the artful Grecian stole.
"On the other side
"Is Galatea's dainty dressing-room,
"Wrought in the living marble; and within
"Is seen the fountain where she used to twine
"The ringlets on her neck that did ensnare
"The melancholy Cyclop."—But what care you,
A soldier, for such fantasies?   I know
A way that better shall persuade you to
That place for our sweet marriage residence:—
There Damon hath his villa—Ha! you seem
Determined by the fast proximity
Of such a friendship, more than all my love.
    Pyth. Does Damon dwell there?
    Cal. No; his Hermion
And his young boy—Oh! 'tis a beauteous child!—
Are sent there from the city's noxious air;
And he doth visit them whene'er the state
Gives him brief respite.   Tell me, Pythias,
Shall we not see the hymeneal moon
Glide through the blue heavens there?

Pyth. My own adored one!
If thou should'st bid me sail away with thee
To seek the isles of the Hesperides,
I would, with such a pilot, spread my sail
Beyond the trophies of great Hercules,
Making thine eyes my Cynosure!

Enter LUCULLUS, *hastily.*

How now, Lucullus?
  Luc. Where is my lord? I was informed
That I should find him here—a senator
Bade me require him instantly.
  Pyth. He waits here
To attend us to the temple, and if things
Of weight demand his ear, you'll find him yonder
In the pale cypress-grove.   [*Exit Lucullus.*
Nothing, I hope,
Has happened to withdraw him from the rite
That makes thee mine.
  Cal. I hope not.—Who is this
That seeks him out so earnestly?
  Pyth. He is
A brave Italian, whom the Carthage pirates
Seized on his native coast, and sold a slave.
Damon hath given him back his liberty,
But yet, of his free will, he tends him still;
And more than very freedom doth he hold
The right to serve a man that is fine touched
With a most merciful spirit.
  Cal. Nay, my Pythias,
Make not your friend's high qualities for aye
The burthen of your eloquence.   In sooth,
I should be almost jealous of a steed
I saw you pat with a too liberal hand;
And—ha! he comes.
                    Enter DAMON.

Damon. Pythias—[*Aside.*] I must not let
Calanthe read my purpose.—Calanthe,

The blessing and the bounty of the gods
Be with you, over you, and all around you,
Thou gentle girl! [*Aside to Pythias.*] Pythias, a word with you.
What heard I, think you, Pythias, even now?

   Cal. There has been Pythias, all this forenoon,
Would speak to me of nothing but the esteem
In which he held thee, Damon.

   Damon. What! no word
Touching the quality of that foolish love
He bears the fair Calanthe? [*Aside to Pythias.*] We are undone,
We and our wretched city, Pythias!

   Pyth. [*Aside to Damon.*] What dost thou mean?

   Cal. No, not a single word—
Thou, thou alone mad'st up his eulogy.

   Damon. What think'st thou, Pythias? A king!   [*Aside.*

   Pyth. [*Aside to Damon.*] What! who?

   Damon. [*To Calanthe.*] Heed not
His silken praises of me. [*Aside to Pythias.*] Dionysius
Is to be crownéd in the senate-house.

   Pyth. Can it be possible?

   Damon. I say thee yea—
His soldiers line the streets.

   Pyth. But will the senate—
The coward senate, sanction it? Will none
Oppose him in it?

   Damon. Oppose him!—[*Aloud.*] All the gods
So help or strike me, as I will oppose him!
Let Ætna vomit fire upon his side,
And I alone,—[*Searching about him.*] Have I forgot my dagger!

   Cal. How now, my Pythias?

   Pyth. He is moved, Calanthe,
By some most urgent matter of the state;
Nay, heed him not!

   Damon. Pythias, as I intended
To be a witness to thy wedding rite,
I did not bear a weapon—give me thy poniard.

   Pyth. Speak, to what end?

   Damon. No matter, give it me.

Cal. Ha! What does he intend.   Now, by my love,
Pythias, I do adjure thee—

Pyth. Whither, Damon,
Where would'st thou go?

Damon. Unto the senate-house.

Pyth. Then I will with you, too.

Cal. He shall not!

Damon. No!   [*To Calanthe.*
Thou say'st aright,—he shall not!   Fair Calanthe,
This is no hour to leave thee!   What, Calanthe,
Should bridegrooms give the law, and 'gin to rule
Even on their wedding day?   I charge thee, sweet,
Assert thy brief dominion while thou canst:
'Twill speedily be his turn.   [*Aside to Pythias.*
It shall not be!   It is against the law
For any soldier in the senate-house
To lift his helm of war, and what avail
Were thy companionship!   Calanthe, take him,
Take him away, and heaven be o'er you both!

Pyth. But thou wilt promise me, upon the faith
Of an old friendship, that thy sudden hand
Will not attempt a rashness?

Damon. Be thou satisfied;
I will do naught in passion.   Come, Calanthe,   [*Aside.*
Assert thy right in him, and take him hence
Unto the garden-walk, and tell him o'er
The names of all thy favorite plants: I pray thee,
Keep him in busy trifles till the hour
For the sweet rite be come—[*Joins their hands*]—That's
      well, my girl;
There, take him by the arm!

Cal. Come, Pythias, come!
I thank thee, Damon, for thy tender counsel.

Pyth. Nay, Damon—nay, Calanthe—

Cal. Nay me no nays;
I say it shall be so.

Damon. May the gods pour
Their blessing o'er your heads!—Farewell! farewell!

I have no time to bide here, but my heart
Shall be beside you at the altar place.
Perhaps it is an idle fear compels me
Hence from your sight: I will if possible
Return and see you wedded.   Fare you well!
                    [*Exeunt Pythias, and Calanthe.*
Now, Syracuse, for thee!—And may the fates
So bless, or curse me, as I act in this!   [*Exit.*

SCENE II.—*The Senate-House of Syracuse.*

SENATORS *assembled*—PHILISTIUS *at their head.*—DIONYSIUS
    standing.—DAMOCLES *seated near him.*

Dam. So soon warned back again!

Dion. So soon, good fathers.
My last despatches here set forth that scarce
I had amassed and formed our gallant legions
When, as by magic, word of the precaution
Was spirited to their camp—and on the word
These Carthaginians took their second thought,
And so fell back.

Phil. I do submit to you,
That out of this so happy consequence
Of Dionysius' movement on the citadel,
Not only is his pardon for the act
Freely drawn forth, but we are called upon
Our thanks most manifestly to express
For such a noble service.

Dion. Good Philistius,
I am a soldier; yours and the state's servant,
And claim no notice for my duty done
Beyond the doing it—and the best thanks
I merit, or can have, lie in the issue
Which has most happily resulted.

Dam. [*Rising.*] Nay,
It rests in us to say so.

Phil. Dionysius,
The work which of this enterprise thou hast made,
Proves that our citadel and its resources

Have been misused; and never so controlled
And ordered for our good as by thyself;
Therefore retain it, govern and direct it.—
Would the whole state were like the citadel!
In hot and angry times like these, we want
Even such a man.

    Dam.   I, from my heart, assent to
And second this proposal.

    Dion. Most reverend fathers—

    Dam. We pray thee, silence, noble Dionysius!
All here do know what your great modesty
Will urge you to submit; but I will raise
This envious veil wherein you shroud yourself.
It is the time to speak; our country's danger
Calls loudly for some measure at our hands,
Prompt and decisive.

    Damon. [*From without.*] Thou most lowly minion!
I'll have thee whipped for it, and by the head
Made less even than thou art!

Enter DAMON.

    Phil. Who breaks so rude and clamorously in
To scare our grave deliberations?

    Damon. A senator!—First let me ask you why,
Upon my way here to sit down with you,
I have encountered in the open streets,
Nay, at the very threshold of your doors,
Soldiers and satellites arrayed and marshalled
With their swords out? Why have I been obstructed
By an armed bandit in my peaceful walk here,
To take my rightful seat in the senate-house?
Why has a ruffian soldier privilege
To hold his weapon to my throat? A tainted,
Disgraced, and abject traitor, Procles! Who
Dared place the soldiers round the senate-house?

    Phil. I pray you, fathers, let not this rash man
Disturb the grave and full consideration
Of the important matter, touching which

We spoke ere he rushed in.

Dam. [*To the Senators.*] I did require
To know from you, without a hand or head,
Such as to us hath been our Dionysius
What now were our most likely fate?

Damon. The fate
Of freeman, in the full, free exercise
Of all the noble rights that freeman love!
Free in our streets to walk; free in our councils
To speak and act—

Phil. I do entreat you, senators,
Protect me from this scolding demagogue.

Damon. Demagogue, Philistius!
Who was the demagogue, when at my challenge
He was denounced and silenced by the senate,
And your scant oratory spent itself
In fume and vapor?

Dam. Silence, Damon, silence!
And let the council use its privilege.

Damon. Who bids me silence? Damocles, the soft
And pliant willow, Damocles! But come,
What do you dare propose? Come, I'll be silent—
Go on.

Phil. Resolve you, then, is Dionysius
This head indeed to us? Acting for us—
Yea, governing, that long have proved we cannot,
Although we feign it, govern for ourselves!

Dam. Then who so fit, in such extremity,
To be the single pillar, on whose strength
All power should rest?

Phil. Ay, and what needs the state
Our crowded and contentious councils here?
And therefore, senators—countrymen, rather,
That we may be wiser and better ruled
Than by ourselves we are; that the state's danger
May be confronted boldly, and that he
May have but his just meed, I do submit
That forthwith we dissolve ourselves, and choose
A king in Dionysius.

Damon. King! A King?

1st Sen. I do approve it.

2d Sen. Ay, and I.

Dam. And all! All are content!

Damon. And all! are all content?
A nation's right betrayed,
And all content! Oh, slaves! oh, parricides!
Oh, by the brightest hope a just man has,
I blush to look around and call you men!
What! with your own free, willing hands yield up
The ancient fabric of your constitution,
To be a garrison, a common barrack,
And common guard-house, and for common cut-throats?
What! will ye all combine to tie a stone
Each to each other's neck, and drown like dogs
Within the tide of time, and never float
To after ages, or, at best, but float
A buoyant pestilence? Can ye but dig
Your own dark graves, creep into them, and die?

3d Sen. I have not sanctioned it.

4th Sen. Nor I.

5th Sen. Nor I.

Damon. Oh! thanks for these few voices! but, alas!
How lonely do they sound! Do you not all
Start up at once, and cry out liberty?
Are you so bound in fetters of the mind,
That there you sit, as if you were yourselves
Incorporate with the marble? Syracusans!—
But no! I will not rail, nor chide, nor curse ye!
I will implore you, fellow-countrymen,
With blinded eyes, and weak and broken speech,
I will implore you—Oh! I am weak in words,
But I could bring such advocates before you!
Your father's sacred images; old men,
That have been grandsires; women with their children
Caught up in fear and hurry, in their arms—
And those old men should lift their shivering voices
And palsied hands—and those affrighted mothers

Should hold their innocent infants forth, and ask,
Could you make slaves of them?
  Phil. I dissolve the senate
At its own vote and instance.
  Dam. And all hail!
Hail, Dionysius, King of Syracuse!
  Dion. Is this the vote?
  Damon. There is no vote! Philistius,
Hold you your seat; keep in your places, senators.
  Dion. I ask, is this the vote?
  Phil. It is the vote,
My gracious liege and sovereign.
  Damon. I say, nay!
You have not voted, Naxillus, nor Petus—
Nor you, nor you, nor you—
  Phil. In my capacity,
As head and organ of the city council,
I do asseverate it is the vote!
All hail, then, Dionysius!
  [*They all kneel to Dionysius except Damon and the Senators who
    have voted in the negative.*
  Dion. I thank you, friends and countrymen, I thank ye!
  Damon. Oh! all the gods, my country, oh, my country!
  Dion. And that we may have leisure to put on
With fitting dignity our garb of power,
We do now, first assuming our own right,
Command from this, that was the senate-house,
Those rash, tumultuous men, who still would tempt
The city's peace with wild vociferation
And vain contentious rivalry.   [*Pointing to Damon.*
Away!
  Damon. I stand,
A senator, within the senate-house!
  Dion. Traitor! and dost thou dare me to my face?
  Damon. Traitor! to whom? to thee!—Oh! Syracuse,
Is this thy registered doom? To have no meaning
For the proud names of liberty and virtue,
But as some regal braggart sets it down

In his vocabulary?   And the sense,
The broad, bright sense that Nature hath assigned them
In her infallible volume, interdicted
Forever from thy knowledge; or, if seen,
And known, and put in use, denounced as treasonable,
And treated thus?   No, Dionysius, no!
I am no traitor!   But in mine allegiance
To my lost country, I proclaim thee one!
    Dion. My guards, there!   Ho!
    Damon. What! hast thou, then, invoked
Thy satellites already?

       Enter PROCLES *and* SOLDIERS.

    Dion. Seize him!
    Damon. [*Rushes on Dionysius and attempts to stab him.*]
        First
Receive a freeman's legacy!   [*He is intercepted by guards and
        Procles.*] Dionysius,
Thy genius is triumphant, and old Syracuse
Bows her to the dust at last!—'Tis done; 'tis o'er,
And we are slaves forever!
    Dion. We reserve
This proud, assassinating demagogue,
Who whets his dagger on philosophy,
For—an example to his cut-throat school!—
The axe, and not the sword.   Out of his blood
We'll mix a cement to our monarchy:
Here do we doom him to a public death!
    Damon. Death's the best gift to one that never yet
Wished to survive his country.   Here are men
Fit for the life a tyrant can bestow!
Let such as these live on.
    Dion. Hold thou there!
Lest, having stirred our vengeance into wrath,
It reach unto those dearer than thyself—
Thy wife and child.
Ha! have I touched thee, Damon?   Is there a way
To level thee unto the feebleness

DIONYSIUS CONDEMNING DAMON TO DEATH.

Of universal nature?   What, no word?
Come, use thy time, my brave philosopher!
Thou hast few moments left!
       Damon. I know thee well—
Thou art wont to use thy tortures on the heart,
Watching its agonizing throbs, and making
A science of that fell anatomy!
These are thy bloody metaphysics—this
Thy barbarous philosophy!   I own
Thou hast struck thy venomed sting into my soul,
But while I'm wounded, I despise thee still!
My wife! my child!   Oh, Dionysius,
Thou shouldst have spared me that!—Procles, lead on.
       [*Procles precedes Damon, who goes out, followed by the
           Guards.—The Senators surround Dionysius—and distant
           shouts are heard, as the scene closes.*

SCENE III.—*A Chamber in Arria's House.—Shouts heard without.*

Enter PYTHIAS.

       Pyth. What shouts rend the wide city?   There is a roar
Deep as the murmuring of Ætna.   Gods!
I tremble for his safety!   What, ho, there!

Enter SERVANT.

Hast thou, sirrah,
Heard no intelligence how matters speed
Up at the senate-house?
       Ser. My lord, no word.
       Pyth. And those time-cheating knaves I sent to know—
They have not yet returned?
       Ser. Not yet, my lord.
       Pyth. Run thither, then—despatch, for thou'rt light-limbed;
Regard Lord Damon well; note how he seems,
And what he says—On, on!
       Ser. My lord, I will.
       Pyth. And, hark!
Observe of all if any words of wrath
Fall between him and Dionysius—
Begone!   [*Exit Servant.*

He is hotly mettled,
And not life's autumn, nor the discipline
Of cold Pythagoras' school, has tamed it yet.

Enter SERVANT.

Ser. My lord—
Pyth. Now, sir, what from the senate-house?
Ser. My lord, I know not of the senate-house.
Pyth. Not, sir! I sent thee thither, did I not?
Ser. Another, sir.   I am despatched to say,
That all the guests and witnesses are come;
And that with them the bride Calanthe waits
To have thy company to the temple.
Pyth. How!
Is it the hour?
Ser. The hour, my lord, is past.   [*Exit Servant.*
Pyth. Did ever man upon his wedding-day
Feel so impatient of the hour arrived
That is to bless him?   But I dare not stir
Till I have tidings of my friend:—he is
Exposed to deadly loss, and may have need
Of Pythias' sword.   By Heaven, I do him wrong
In tarrying from his presence at an hour
So full of peril and perhaps of death.
Death, did I say?   I must—

Enter ARRIA.

Arria. Now, Pythias, Pythias,
Why is it that we wait so long for thee?
Fie! thou a bridegroom! absent now!
Pyth. Gods! if that Dionysius
Should level at his life!—I prithee, Arria,
How soon might one with active and light foot
Run to the senate-house, and back again
From hence?
Arria. Is the man crazed and lunatic?
Is it your pleasure that we wait a season—
I, sir, Calanthe, and our guests and kinsmen,
For your best humor to get wedded in?

Pyth. Good Arria, pardon me; take not amiss
This absent seeming—but I am not well,
I know not how, but so you see it is—
Give me half an hour—nay, the half—the tithe
Of such a time!
    Arria. Pythias, indeed art ill?
    Pyth. I'faith, I am—sick in the head and heart!
Bear with me, Arria; go among our guests,
And cheat their notice of this accident;
I shall be better quickly—well, quite well.
    Arria. The gods forefend it should fall otherwise!   [*Exit.*
    Pyth. Oh, how these leaden-footed limping minutes
Do lag and creep beneath my lashing wish!
When fiery expectation mounts the time,
Time is a spiritless and jaded steed,
That staggers 'neath his rider.   Gracious gods!
Will none of them come to relieve this weight
From my o'erloaded heart!—What shall I do?
Calanthe!
           Enter CALANTHE.

    Cal. My dear Pythias!
    Pyth. Calanthe!
    Cal. My mother whispered me you were not well;
And here, even as you see me, though you should not
Have seen me in my bridal garments thus
Till we were wedded—yet even thus I come
To speak with you, and comfort you, my Pythias.
    Pyth. Beshrew her heart, now, though she be thy mother,
For such ill-timed and womanish whispering!
I am as well as I am happy, love.
    Cal. She said, too, but I heed it not—
    Pyth. What said she?
    Cal. She prayed the gods your sickness might be free
From surfeit sickness; but I heed it not:
You know I heed it not; I cannot think
Your heart is such a bad one, Pythias.
    Pyth. Tears, my Calanthe!   Ah, my own fair girl,
The maiden pulse beating upon thy brow

Is not so faithful to its sister pulse,
Which throbs within this little heart of thine.
As I have been, and am!—Ha! dost thou smile?
Now, by the gods! I cannot see the smile,
And tarry longer from the property
Of this dear hand I grasp.   Come, my Calanthe,
They tarry for us, do they not?
     Cal. They do.
     Pyth. Nay, do not bend thy head, but let me gaze
Upon thee as we go, that those fine looks,
So full of life and joy, may banish from me
The ghastly thought of death!
     Cal. Death!
     Pyth. Nay, forgive me;
I know not what I say.—Ye bounteous gods,
Who guard the good, because yourselves are good,
Wave your protecting arm around him!—Come—
Oh, Friendship! thou must yield it for a time
To the torch-bearer, when he lights his fires
From two such eyes as these are! Come, Calanthe.

[*As they are going,* LUCULLUS *enters hastily.*—*Pythias lets fall
     Calanthe's hand and rushes to him.*

[*To Lucullus.*]· Where, sirrah, where?   Where shall I speak with
          him?
     Luc. He did desire, my Lord, that I should lead you.
     Pyth. And not say where?
     Luc. It was his charge, my lord.
     Pyth. In one word, say the hour and place of this,
Or—ha! I see it in thine eye—his life,
His life is forfeit—he is doomed to death
     Luc. Alas! my lord.
     Pyth. Oh, by the gods, it is so!
And, like a selfish coward, did I stand
And saw him rush and singly front himself
Against a host, when it was evident,
As is the universal light of day,
He must have perished in it—Coward! coward!

He would not thus have done!

Luc. My lord—

Pyth. Speak not—

I know thou would'st admonish me to speed,

Or see him dead.

    Cal. Pythias! Pythias!   *[Grasps his arm.*

    Pyth. Now let me go—away, I say!

    Cal. Pythias!

    Pyth. I say, unloose me, or by all—

Thou art as guilty, with thy blandishments,

That did provoke this ruin, as I am

For being tempted by thee!—Woman, away!   *[Throws her off.*

    Cal. Unkind one!

    Pyth. Ha! thou weepest!—Oh, Calanthe!

Forgive me—pity me—I am desperate!

I know not what I do—but—*[Embraces her.]*—Oh, Calanthe,

There is a horrid fate that tears me hence.

Now, sirrah, lead me on!—Away! away!

    Cal. Pythias! Pythias!

    [Clings to Pythias as he rushes out, preceded by Lucullus.

Scene IV.—*A Dungeon.*

DAMON *discovered at a table, writing.*

Damon. Existence! what is that? a name for nothing!

It is a cloudy sky chased by the winds,—

Its fickle form no sooner chosen than changed!

It is the whirling of the mountain-flood,

Which, as we look upon it, keeps its shape.

Though what composed that shape, and what composes,

Hath passed—will pass—may, and is passing on,

Even while we think to hold it in our eyes,

And deem it there. Fie! fie! a feverish vision,

A crude and crowded dream, unwilled, unbidden,

By the weak wretch that dreams it.   *[Noise of chains and bolts.*

Enter PROCLES *and two Guards.*

    Proc. Damon, thine hour is come.

    Damon. Past, sir, say past—to come, argues a stay

Upon the coming. He has refused me, then,

Your general, Dionysius!—the king—
He has refused me even this little respite
I asked of him?

  Proc. All! he refuses all.

  Damon. Did'st tell him why I asked it?   Did'st explain
It was to have my wife warned here to Syracuse,
From her near dwelling upon Ætna's side,
To see me ere I die?

  Proc. I said it, sir.

  Damon. And he refused it?

  Proc. Ay, sir; he refused.

  Damon. Upon the instant?

  Proc. Yes, upon the instant.

  Damon. Is he not wedded?

  Proc. Yes.

  Damon. A father, too?

  Proc. He is a father, too.

  Damon. And he refused it?
I will attend you, and I pray you pardon—
This is no time to play the catechist.
One little boon I have to beg of thee;
It is the last.   I would not fain be irksome;
It is the last I shall prefer on earth
Unto my fellow-men.   This is my testament:
I pray thee give it to a friend of mine,
Who may inquire about me: he will hold it,
And use it for my wife.

  Proc. His name?

  Damon. It is—
I did not wish to trust my coward tongue
With utterance of that name; I feared it would
Pluck up all manhood by the roots; but, sir,
This now is childish; Pythias, sir!—

      [*Procles retires and talks with the guards.*

Alas!
To-day will prove a woful wedding-day
To thee and thy Calanthe!—And my Hermion,
My fond, poor Hermion, and my boy—
Good Procles,—

Let me not stand here talking idly thus—
I am quite ready—on, sir! I attend you!

> [*Exeunt Procles, Damon, and the guards.*

ACT III.

SCENE I.—*A Street.*

Enter four guards and PROCLES *with* DAMON *in chains, followed
by four more guards.*

Damon. A moment's pause here, Procles.

> [*Procles motions the guards to halt.*

We discoursed together
Of an old friend of mine, who in all likelihood
Would question thee concerning my last thoughts,
While leaving this vain world; I do entreat thee,
When thou shalt see that man, commend me to him,
And say, a certainty of how true a friend
And father he will be unto my wife
And child—

Pyth. Hold back! It is impossible
That ye can butcher him, till we speak together!

Enter PYTHIAS, *preceded by soldiers, who obstruct his way.*

I am his nearest friend! I should receive
His dying words—hold back!   [*Breaks through them.*
Oh, Damon! Damon!

Damon. I wished for this, but feared it, Pythias!
Tush!—we are men, my Pythias; we are men,
And tears do not become us.

Pyth. Doom and death
In the same moment! Is there no hope, Damon?
Is everything impossible?

Damon. For me,
With Dionysius, everything—I craved
But six hours' respite, that my wife may come,
And see me—

Pyth. And he would not?

Damon. Not an hour—
Yet to have kissed her, and my little boy—
Just to have kissed her—
    Pyth. The cold villain!
    Damon. Well,
All that is o'er now, and this talk superfluous.
Ere you came up, my friend, I was about
To leave a greeting for you with the officer;
I bade him say, too—for, despite of rules
Well conned and understood, in such a time
As this—so sudden, hopeless, and unlooked for,—
The eye will water, and the heart grow cowardly,
At thoughts of home, and things we love at home;
And something like a sorrow, or a fear,
For what may happen them, will stick in the throat
To choke our words and make them weak and womanish!
    Pyth. Tears have a quality of manhood in them,
When shed for what we love.
    Damon. I bade him say,
That half my fear for her, and my young boy,
As to their future fate, was banished,
In the full certainty I felt of all
The care and kindness thou wilt have of them
    Pyth. That was a true thought, Damon.
    Damon. Pythias, I know it.
And when the shock of this hath passed away,
And thou art happy with thy sweet Calanthe—
    Pyth. Damon!
    Damon. Well, Pythias?
    Pyth. Did'st thou not say
It was thy last desire to look upon
Thy wife and child, before—
    Damon. I would give up,—
Were my life meted out by destiny
Into a thousand years of happiness,—
All that long measure of felicity,
But for a single moment, in the which
I might compress them to my heart.

Pyth. Good Procles,
Lead me at once to Dionysius—
I mean, unto the king—that's his new name—
Lead me unto the king—[*Trumpet is heard.*] Ha! here he comes!

Enter DIONYSIUS *and* DAMOCLES.

Behold me, Dionysius, at thy feet!   [*Kneels.*
As thou dost love thy wife, and thy sweet children;
As thou'rt a husband and a father, hear me!
Let Damon go and see his wife and child
Before he dies—for four hours respite him—
Put me in chains: plunge me into his dungeon,
As pledge for his return; do this—but this—
And may the gods themselves build up thy greatness
As high as their own heaven.   [*Rises.*
    Dion. What wonder's this?
Is he thy brother?
    Pyth. No, not quite my brother!
Not—yes, he is—he is my brother!
    Dion. Damon—is this a quibble of thy school?
    Damon. No quibble, for he is not so in kin,
Not in the fashion that the word puts on,
But brother in the heart!
    Dion. [*To Damon.*] Didst urge him on
To this?
    Pyth. By the gods, no!
    Dion. And should I grant
Thy friend's request, leaving thee free to go,
Unwatched, unguarded, thou mak'st naught of it;
Quite sure that thou wilt come and ransom him,
At the imminent time?
    Damon. Sure of it? Hearest thou, Heaven?
The emptiest things reverberate most sound,
And hollow hearts have words of boisterous promise.
I can say only—I am sure!
    Dion. 'Tis granted.
    [*Two officers take the chains off Damon, and place them on
        Pythias.*
How far abides thy wife from hence?

Damon. Four leagues.

Dion. For six hours we defer thy death.   'Tis now
The noon exactly; and at the sixth hour
See that thou stand'st not far from him; away!
Conduct that man to prison.

Damon. Farewell, Pythias!

Pyth. And farewell, Damon!   Not a word upon it.
Speed thee.   What, tears?—Forbear.

Damon. I did not think
To shed one tear; but friendship like to thine—

Pyth. Farewell!   Come, officer.

Damon. I pray thee, Procles,
Give me the testament thou hadst of me.   [*Procles gives it to him.*
Pythias, thy hand again: Pythias, farewell!

Pyth. Farewell!
                    [*Exeunt Damon, Pythias, Procles, and guards.*

Dion. Oh, by the wide world, Damocles,
I did not think the heart of man was moulded
To such a purpose.

Dam. It is wondrous.

Dion. Wondrous!
Sir, it doth win from the old imaginers
Their wit and novelty!—
I'll visit Pythias in his dungeon: get me
A deep disguise.   We'll use such artifice
As the time, and our own counsel, may suggest.—
If they should triumph, crowns are nothingness—
Glory is sound—and grandeur, poverty!   [*Exeunt.*

SCENE II.—*Another Street.*

Enter DAMON *and* LUCULLUS.

Luc. Oh, my dear lord, my master, and my friend,
The sight of you thus safe—

Damon. Safe!

Luc. For at least
A respite, my kind lord.

Damon. No more, Lucullus.
Is my horse ready?

Luc. Yes, the gallant grey,
Of Anaxagoras, you lately purchased.   [*Exit.*

Enter CALANTHE.

Cal. Hold, sir!—is what they tell me true?
Damon. Calanthe,
At any time save this thy voice would have
The power to stay me.—Prithee, let me pass—
Nor yet abridge me of that fleeting space
Given to my heart.
    Cal. Speak! have they said the truth!
Have you consented to put in the pledge
Of Pythias' life for your return?
    Damon. 'Tis better
That I should say to her—'Hermion, I die?'
Than that another should hereafter tell,
'Damon is dead!'
    Cal. No! you would say to her,
'Pythias has died for me'—even now the citizens
Cried in mine ear, 'Calanthe, look to it!'
    Damon. And do you think I would betray him!
    Cal. Think of it?
I give no thought upon it—Possibility,
Though it should weigh but the least part of a chance
Is quite enough—Damon may let him die—
Ay, meanly live himself, and let him die!
    Damon. Calanthe, I'll not swear.   When men lift up
Their hands unto the gods, it is to give
Assurance to a doubt: But to confirm,
By any attestation, the return
Of Damon unto Pythias, would profane
The sanctity of friendship—Fare the well.—   [*She clings to him.*
Nay, cling not to me.
    Cal. So will Hermion cling—
But Damon will not so reject her.
She will implore thee back to life again,
And her loud cries will pierce thy inmost breast,
And Pythias will be murdered!
    Damon. I must unloose thy grasping.

Cal. Mercy, Damon!

Damon. Unwillingly I stay thy struggling hands—
Forgive me for't.

Cal. Damon, have mercy on me!

Damon. May the gods bless thee!   [*Exit.*

Cal. Damon, mercy, Damon!
He flies!—and there's a voice that from my heart,
As from the grave cries out, that never more
He will return to Pythias.—Hermion—his child—
And his own selfish instinct—or some accident
May fall, and stay him back, and that will be
The axe to Pythias!—Oh, I will follow him—
I'll tell him that; and, like a drowning wretch,
Fasten about his neck, and cling to him!
But, ah!—he flies—his steed is on the wind!
My evil demon wings him, and he tramps
Already the wide distance!—Pythias,
The flowers in bridal mockery on my brow,
Thus I rend off, and keep them for the grave!

Enter DIONYSIUS, *disguised.*

Dion. Thy name's Calanthe, and thou art the bride
Of Pythias—is't not thus?

Cal. What dost thou come
To say to me of Pythias?

Dion.   Art thou not
His bride?

Cal. The marriage-temple was prepared,
The virgins' voices were sent up to Heaven,
When death did all at once
Rise up, and all that pomp did disappear,
And for the altar, I behold the tomb—
He never will return!

Dion. He will not.

Cal. Ha!
Dost thou confirm my apprehensions?
They were black enough already—and thy smile—
It is the gloss upon the raven's plumes—
Thy smile is horrible!

PYTHIAS IN PRISON.

Dion. Calanthe, hear me:
The tyrant Dionysius has resolved
To intercept this Damon, and prevent
His coming back to Syracuse.
    Cal. Oh, gods!
    Dion. I am an inmate in the tyrant's house,
And learned his fell decree!
    Cal. Then speed thee hence:
Mount thou the fleetest steed in Syracuse—
Pursue the unhappy Damon—tell him this:
I know he has a brave and generous nature,
Will not betray his friend! Go after him,
And save my husband!
    Dion. I have found a way
To rescue him already: thou and Pythias
Shall fly from Syracuse.
    Cal. What! shall he 'scape
The tyrant's fangs?
    Dion. Forever!—But thou must
Follow my precept.
    Cal. I will obey you, sir,
And bless you!
    Dion. Then to Pythias—come with me.   [*Exeunt.*

SCENE III.—*A terrace attached to the prison, with the sea outstretched before it.—A portal on one side—on the other side, the dungeon-door of Pythias, barred and chained.*

Enter DIONYSIUS, *preceded by* PROCLES, *who points to the dungeon.*

    Dion. Is this the dungeon?—Unbar the door.—
        [*Procles undraws the bolts and lets fall the chains.*
I'll probe him deeply.—
Now observe well the orders that I gave thee!
    [*Motions him away and opens the door.—Exit Procles.*
My lord, Pythias!
    Pyth. [*Within.*] How now! who calls me?
    Dion. A friend, Pythias: the time is precious; haste,
And follow me.

Enter PYTHIAS, *from dungeon.*

Pyth. Where do you lead me?

Dion. I come
To serve and succor thee.

Pyth. And who art thou?
And how canst succor me?

Dion. I dwell beneath
The tyrant's roof, and learned by accident
This fell determination—he hath resolved—

Pyth. My life!

Dion. Thy life!
Ere this, he hath dispatched some twenty men
To intercept thy friend on his approach
To meet and ransom thee.

Pyth. Almighty Heaven!

Dion. He not arriving at the appointed hour,
Thy life is forfeited.

Pyth. We try the depth together; I had hoped
That one or other of us could have lived
For thy poor Hermion's, or Calanthe's sake—
No matter.

Dion. Pythias, I came to save thee.

Pyth. What dost thou mean?

Dion. Urged by my pity for such noble friends,
So trusting and betrayed—anxious, besides,
To leave the tyrant's court,
Hither I bribed my way.—Thy fair Calanthe
Shall be the partner of thy flight.—Thy father—

Pyth. Sir!

Dion. Yes, thy father, too—thy time-struck father,
Who, till this day, for many circling years
Hath not held human intercourse,
Was visited by me—he hath upraised him
From his lonely bed.

Pyth. Thou speak'st of miracles!

Dion. And ere I came, with all dispatch and secrecy,
I have provided in the port of Syracuse
A good, quick-sailing ship—yonder she lies,

Her sails already spread before the breeze,
And thou and thy Calanthe—see, she comes—
Haste, lady, haste to thy betrothéd lord!
Pyth. Wide-working Heaven, Calanthe?

Enter CALANTHE.

Cal. Pythias!
Though, when thou should'st have cherished, thou did'st spurn
        me,—
Though, in the holy place where we had met
To vow ourselves away unto each other,—
Though there, when I was kneeling at thy feet,
Thou didst forswear and mock at me—yet here
I do forgive thee all—and I will love thee
As never woman loved her young heart's idol.
So thou but speed'st to safety!
    Pyth. Hold, Calanthe.—
If mothers love the babe upon the breast,
When it looks up with laughter in his eyes,
Making them weep for joy—if they can love,
I loved, and do love thee, my own Calanthe:
But wert thou magnified above thyself,
As mnch in fascination as thou art
Above all creatures else—by all the gods,
In awful reverence sworn, I would not cheat
My honor!
    Cal. How!
    Dion. Madam, what dost intend?
    Pyth. Dost thou not know the tyrant spared his life
On the security I gave for him?
Stand I not here his pledge?
    Dion. [*Aside.*] 'Tis wonderful!
His brow is fixed; his eye is resolute.
    Cal. Pythias, mine idolized and tender Pythias,
Am I then scorned?
    Dion. The tyrant doth break faith with thee.
    Pyth. 'Tis said so.
    Cal. And Damon cannot come to be thy ransom.
    Pyth. I have heard it, my Calanthe.

Cal. And that thou—
That thou—Oh, gods!—must die when he comes not!
　　Pyth. And that I know, Calanthe.
　　Cal. If thou knowest it,
What is thy heart, then, that it can still be obstinate?
　　Pyth. I should not have heard it; or, having heard it,
I still may hold it false.　This busy world
Is but made up of slight contingencies—
There are a thousand that may alter this,
Or leave it where it was; there is not one
Should push us a mere point from any pledge
Of manliness and honor!
Yet would I live!
Live to possess my own Calanthe here,
Who recommends existence with a smile
So sad and beautiful!—Yet would I live—
But not dishonored!—Still, Calanthe, he *may* return:
May! may!—That word ends all!　Death looks but grimly,
And the deep grave is cheerless—yet I do—
I do prefer the certainty of death
Unto the possibility of dishonor!
　　Dion. Behold!　Behold!　　　　　　　*[Pointing off.*
The good ship hath her streaming signal out!
The canvas swells up to the wooing wind!
The boat puts off—now, now, or never!
　　Cal. See
How swiftly, in her gallant liberty,
She comes through the calm sea!—Oh, hark! the oars
How rapidly they plash in harmony!
Oh, look at Freedom, Pythias, look at it!
How beautiful it is upon the sea!
Pythias, my Pythias—Oh! how we shall laugh
While bounding o'er the blessed wave that bears us
From doom and death, to some fair Grecian isle!
　　Dion. See, they approach! dost hesitate?
　　Cal. Pythias!—my husband, Pythias!
　　Pyth. No! no! so help me heaven!—'Tis hard!
It plucks my heart up—but, no! no!

Cal. Oh, gods!

[*Pythias rushes into the dungeon—Calanthe falls into the arms of Dionysius.*

ACT IV.

SCENE I.—*A garden.—A table with fruit laid out.*

HERMION *discovered arranging a little feast.—Her* CHILD *beside her, with a basket of flowers.*

Child. Will he come soon home, mother?

Her. I pray the gods
He may, my child.

Child. It seems so long a time
Since he has ta'en me on his knee, and kissed me.

Her. Hark thee, my boy!
This is the hour wherein Lucullus said
Thy father would arrive to visit us.
Go, see if he be coming; he'll be glad
To greet the rosy fruit upon thy cheeks,
Even as he enters our sweet garden here.
Hie thee, and bear me word if he approaches—
The first kiss shall be thine.   [*Exit Child.*
Thou unkind Damon!
To send me here to woman's loneliness,
A prey to all the sickening hopes and fears
I must have of thee, in these blustering times.

Enter DAMON *with the* CHILD *in his arms.*

Child. See, I have found him for you, mother!

Her. Ha!

Damon. Hermion! my treasure, Hermion!

Her. My dear lord!
I had prepared this little feast for you,
But hope at last grew sick within my heart,
And I could hardly force it to a thought
That yet thou wouldst arrive.   Oft I looked out
Upon the weary way thou shouldst have journeyed,

And oft the hills' dim vapor rose like Damon,
Till the sun came to shape it, and to show me
That yet thou wert away.

Damon. And are ye, then,
Are ye so helpless in our absence, Hermion?

Her. Come, now—you know it. Oh, my dear, dear husband!
If I should tell thee of my quaking heart,
While thou art bustling there in Syracuse—
Why wilt thou start?—'twould cheat thee of thy tears,
And make thee womanish; and—for I know
Thou lov'st thy own poor Hermion—thou shouldst swear
Never again to leave her.

Damon. Nerve me, Heaven!

Her. Indeed thou shouldst! and look thee here, my Damon!
But for this little boy, here, and his talk,—
His childish prattle on my knee, of what
He would achieve and be—Come, sir, rehearse
These matters over; say, what wouldst thou be?

Damon. What wouldst thou be, my boy?

Child. A soldier, father.

Damon. Come, come, now, not a soldier.

Child. Nay, but I'd choose, sir,
To be what Pythias is.

Damon. [*Much moved.*] Thou'rt a brave boy!
Go pluck a flower from yonder gay recess,
At the other end of the garden. Wreathe me now
The fairest garland for my welcome—there—
A brave, brave boy!—   [*Exit Child.*
[*Aside.*] Now, gods!

Her. Dost thou not think
He grows apace?

Damon. Have I in all my life
Given thee an angry look, or word, or been
Ever an unkind mate, my Hermion?

Her. Never! the gods know, never!

Damon. From thy heart
Thou sayest this?

Her. Yea, from my inmost heart.

Damon. I am glad of it; for thou wilt think of this
When I am dead, my Hermion, and 'twill make thee
The kindest mother to our boy!

Her. Oh, gods!
Why dost thou talk of death? Damon, thy cheek,
Thy lip is quivering—art sick or grieved
With some discomfiture? Oh, these wild wars
And bickerings of the state—how have they robbed thee
Of thy soul's quiet.

Damon. Tell me, tell me, Hermion,—
Suppose I should impart the heaviest news
That could possess thine ear: how wouldst thou bear it?

Her. Laugh at it!—mock at it, to make thee smile,
And teach thee to be happy in despite
Of any turn of fortune. What dost thou mean?
What heavy news? I know the part thou takest
In the state's service. Hath the tyrant risen?

Damon. He hath; but that's not it.

Her. The Carthaginians
Have sacked the city?

Damon. No!

Her. Why, then, thy friend,
So well beloved of thee—Pythias!—'Tis he!

Damon, No, thank the gods, not he!

Her. What is it, then?—
The heaviest news that could possess mine ear!—
Ha! 'tis thyself—some danger hath befallen thee,
Or threatens thee.—Speak, my dear Damon, speak,
Or I shall die of thoughts that come to kill me!

Damon. When I wooed thee, Hermion,
'Twas not the fashion of thy face, or form—
Though from the hand of Heaven thou camest so rich
In all external loveliness—it was not
Such excellence that riveted my heart,
And made me thine; but I said to myself
Thus :—Here is one, who, haply were I wrecked
Or, were I to-morrow, or a later day,
Struck down by fortune—

Her. Wert thou made as low
From what thou art as earth's foundation-stone
Is from the top of Ætna—did men scorn thee—
   Damon. Nay, thus I said, my Hermion :—Did their scorn
Fall deadly as it might—here is a woman
Who hath such firm devotion in her love,
She would not rend my heart, but for my sake,—
And, should we have a child, for his sake, too—
Bear firmly up, though death itself—
   Her. Death! Death!
   Damon. [*Giving the Testament.*] Take this—read this—'twill
      speak what I cannot!
I thought I could, and by the gods I cannot!
   Her. Ha! here's a poisoning adder in this scroll—
It eats into my heart!—Die! Damon! Death!
When? how? I cannot understand it—Die!
Where? what offence?
   Damon. I have been doomed to death by Dionysius.
   Her. But thou hast 'scaped the sentence; thou art here
Alone! unguarded!—It is but to fly
To Greece, or Italy, or anywhere
From this.
   Damon. From this to Syracuse.—I'll tell thee:
Ere now I had been dead—
   Her. No! no!
   Damon. Ere this
I had been dead, but that my friend, my Pythias,
By putting on my fetters—giving up
Himself as hostage for my sure return,—
Wrought on the tyrant to bestow me time
To see thee here.
   Her. By the wide world, thou shalt not!
I hold thee here—these arms encompass thee
As doth thy heart its life-spring!
   Damon. Not!
   Her. Thou shalt not!
   Damon. Not! not return!—Not go to take my friend
Out of the fetters I have hung upon him?

DAMON'S FAREWELL.

Her. Life! to save that, the wrong becomes the right.
The gods that made us have so quickened us,
Nature so prompts us, and all men forgive it,
Because all men would do it. By the love—
If thou hast any—of thy wife and child— [*Kneels.*
Ay, frown—

Enter CHILD, *with flowers.*

Do Damon, frown, and kill me, too,
Or live for us! [*Sees the Child, who is approaching her.*
Ha! the blessed gods have sent thee
With thy sweet helplessness—Kneel down, my child,
Hold up thy little hands with mine, and pray
Not to be made an orphan—not so soon,
So very soon!—Kind Damon, look upon us!
Husband, look on us, we are at thy feet!
    Damon. Ye are!—I see it, and my heart bleeds for you.
Nay, I must turn my eyes away from you
While you are urging me to my dishonor,
And bid me murder him that I may live!
Hermion, farewell! [*Turning round and embracing her.*
    Her. [*In agony.*] Live, Damon! live! live! live!
    [*Swoons in his arms.*
    Damon. Hermion, my life, look up! awake, my Hermion!
The hour is past! I trifle with necessity!
Hermion! I now indeed must part from thee,
All pale, and cold, and death-like as thou art:
Thus may I part from thee, to go and be
Myself full soon as cold!— [*Places Hermion on the garden bench.*
Ah! let me hold thee from the earth, and say
With what a broken-hearted love I press thee
For the last time! [*Kissing her.*] Farewell, farewell, forever!
Once more!
    Child. Father, father!
    Damon. My child, too!—Oh, this is too much!
My little orphan!—my dear boy! the gods,
The gods will take my care of thee, my child!
    [*Places Child near Hermion, and rushes out.*

SCENE II.—*The Exterior of Damon's Villa.*

Enter LUCULLUS.

Luc. It is accomplished! I have slain his horse!
Never shall he return! This hand has cast
An intercept between him and the block!
Perchance he'll kill me—but I heed not that:—
The time shall be, when, at Lucullus's name,
He will lift up his hands, and weep for me.
Ha! while I speak, he comes! In desperate haste,
He rushes from the garden! Shall I fly
From the swift fury will await upon
The terrible revealment?—'Tis too late!

Enter DAMON.

Damon. 'Tis o'er, Lucullus; bring thou forth my horse!
I have stayed too long, Lucullus, and my speed
Must leave the winds behind me. By the gods,
The sun is rushing down the west!
    Luc. My lord—
Damon. Why dost thou tremble? Fetch the color back
Into thy cheek, man, nor let thy weak knees
Knock on each other in their cowardice!
Time flies—be brief—go bring my horse to me!
Be thou as swift as speech, or as my heart is!
    Luc. My lord!—
Damon. Why, slave, dost hear me?
My horse, I say! The hour is past already,
Whereon I bade old Neucles summon me.
    Luc. My generous master, do not slay me!
    Damon. Slave!
Art mad? or dost thou mock me in the last
And most fearful extremity?—Yet you speak not!
    Luc. You were ever kind and merciful, nor yet
Commended me unto the cruel whip,
And I did love you for it!
    Damon. Where's my horse?
    Luc. When I beheld the means of saving you,
I could not hold my hand—my heart was in it,

And in my heart, the hope of giving life
And liberty to Damon; and—
  Damon. Go on!
I am listening to thee!
  Luc. And, in hope to save you.
I slew your steed!
  Damon. Almighty Heavens!
  Luc. Forgive me! ·   [*Kneels.*
  Damon. I am standing here to see if the great gods
Will with their lightning execute my prayer
Upon thee! But thy punishment be mine!
I'll tear thee into pieces!   [*Seizes him.*
  Luc. Spare me! Spare me!
I saved thy life. Oh, do not thou take mine!
  Damon. My friend! my friend! Oh, that the word would
    kill thee!
Pythias is slain!—his blood is on my soul!
He cries, where art thou, Damon? Damon, where art thou?
And Damon's here!—The axe is o'er his neck,—
And in his blood I'm deluged!
  Luc. Spare me! Spare me!
  Damon. A spirit cries, "Revenge and Sacrifice!"
I'll do it—I'll do it—Come—
  Luc. Where should I go?
  Damon. To the eternal river of the dead!
The way is shorter than to Syracuse—
'Tis only far as yonder yawning gulf—
I'll throw thee with one swing to Tartarus,
And follow after thee!—Nay, slave, no struggling!
Pythias is grown impatient! His red ghost
Starts from the ground, and, with a bloody hand,
Waves to the precipice!
  Luc. Have mercy!
  Damon. Call
For mercy on the Furies—not on me!
        [*Exit, dragging Lucullus.*

ACT V.

SCENE I.—*A public place in Syracuse.—A scaffold, with steps ascending to it.—The gates of a prison.—Executioner with an axe, and Guards discovered.*

DAMOCLES *and* PROCLES *discovered.*

Proc. It is a marvellous phantasy, thou speakest of,
In Dionysius.

Dam. Yes, his mind is made
Of strange materials, that are almost cast
In contrariety to one another.
The school and camp, in his ambition, make
A strange division; "with the trumpet's call
"He blends the languor of the poet's lyre!
"The fierce, intrepid captain of the field
"Hath often, on the great Athenian stage,
"Coped with the mightiest monarchs of the Muse;
"And, in mine apprehension, he doth prize
"The applauses of that polished populace
"More than the rising shout of victory.

Proc. "And, over all, that science, which doth hold
"Touching the soul and its affections,
"Its high discoursing, hath attracted him."
It is his creed, that, in this flesh of ours,
Self ever entertains predominance;
And to all friendship he hath ever been
A persevering infidel.   For this,
Belike, he tries a strange experiment.
What sayest thou?   Will Damon come again?

Dam. "Our love of life is in the very instinct
"Of mere material action, when we do
"Even so slight a thing as wink an eye
"Against the wind.   Place me a soulless dog
"Upon the bare edge of a height, and he
"Shall shudder and shrink back, though none have proved
"To his capacity that the fall were dangerous."
I hold the thing impossible.

Proc. He'll not!

Dam. What, when he feels his pent-up soul abroad,
His limbs unfettered, "and the mountain-breeze
"Of liberty all around him, and his life
"Or death upon his own free choice dependent?"
'Tis visionary!

Proc. But is there no hope
Of Dionysius' mercy?

Dam. He'll not give
A second's hundredth part to take a chance in.
"His indignation swells at such a rashness,
"That, in its fling of proud philosophy,
"Can make him feel so much out-soared and humbled."
What a vast multitude upon the hills
Stretch their long blackening outline in the round
Of the blue heavens!

Proc. They wait the great event.
"Mute expectation spreads its anxious hush
"O'er the wide city, that as silent stands
"As its reflection in the quiet sea."
Behold upon the roof what thousands gaze
Toward the distant road that leads to Syracuse!
An hour ago a noise was heard afar,
Like to the pulses of the restless surge;
But as the time approaches, all grows still
As the wide dead of midnight!

Calanthe. [*Without.*] There's no power
Shall stay me back! I must behold him die,
Then follow him!

Enter CALANTHE, *followed by* ARRIA.

Arria. My child!

Cal. I cannot hear thee!
The shrieking of the Furies drowns thy cries!

Arria. This is no place for thee—no place, Calanthe,
For such a one as thou!

Cal. No other place
Is fit for such a wretch! I am his wife
Betrothéd, though not married. There's no place

For me but at his side : in life or death
There is no other.
There is the scaffold with the block on it!
There is the—Oh, good gods !

Arria. Come back, my child!
" Good Damocles, give me your aid to bear
" This wretched woman hence.

Cal. " Oh, mother, mother,
" I'll not be grudged that horrible delight !
" I'll take one long and maddening look of him,
" Whom in the morn I thought I should have waited,
" Blushing within the chamber of a bride,
" And with a heart all full of love and fear.
" Now I await him in a different place,
" And with a cheek that ne'er shall blush again ;
" Whose marble may be spotted o'er with blood,
" But not with modesty : love yet remains,
" But fear, its old companion's fled away,
" And made room for despair !''

Enter DIONYSIUS, *still in disguise.*

Ha ! are you come ?
'Twas you that told me so,
And froze the running currents in my bosom,
To one deep cake of ice ! You said too well
That Damon would not come.—The selfish traitor !
The traitor Damon !

Dion. Hark thee, Calanthe !
It was an idle tale I told to thee !

Cal. Ha !

Dion. A mere coinage, an invention.

Cal. I do not ask thee why that tale was framed—
Framed in thy cold, deliberate cruelty—
But only this one question:—May he yet—
May Damon yet return?

Dion. He may—he is
As free to come, or stay, as are the winds,

Cal. And Dionysius withholds him not?

Dion. He does not.

DAMON RETURNING TO SYRACUSE.

Cal. Whatsoe'er thou art, the gods,
For that one word, be unto thee and thine
Guardians forever!—Oh, that ray of hope
That breaks upon my soul is worth a flood
Of the sweet daylight of Elysium!
Damon may yet return!—But, powers of Heaven!
Death is prepared already!—What is the time?

Dion. Thou may'st perceive by yonder dial-plate
Against the temple, six poor minutes only
Are left for his return.

Cal. And yet he comes not!
Oh, but that temple, where the shade of time
Moves unrelentingly, is dedicate
To the great Goddess of Fidelity—
She will not, in the face of her high fane,
Let such a profanation hurl forever
The altars of her worship to the ground;
For who will offer incense to her name
If Damon's false to Pythias? [*Sound of chains and bolts.*
Ha! they unbar
The ponderous gates!—There is a clank of chains!
They are leading him to death!

Dam. Bring forth the prisoner!

The gates of the prison are flung open, and PYTHIAS *is discovered.
He advances to the scaffold.*

Cal. Pythias!

Pyth. Calanthe here! [*She rushes into his arms.*] My poor
    fond girl!
Thou art the first to meet me at the block,
Thou'lt be the last to leave me at the grave!
How strangely things go on in this bad world—
This was my wedding-day; but for the bride,
I did not think of such a one as death!
I deemed I should have gone to sleep to-night—
This very night—not on the earth's cold lap—
But, with as soft a bosom for my pillow,
And with as true and fond a heart-throb in it
To lull me to my slumber, as e'er yet

Couched the repose of love.   It was, indeed,
A blissful sleep to wish for!
    Cal. Oh, my Pythias,
He yet may come!
    Pyth. Calanthe, no!   Remember
That Dionysius hath prevented it.
    Cal. That was an idle tale of this old man,
And he may yet return!
    Pyth. May yet return!
Speak!—how is this? return!—Oh, life, how strong
Thy love is in the hearts of dying men!
[*To Dionysius.*] Thou'rt he; didst say the tyrant would **prevent**
His coming back to Syracuse?
    Dion. I wronged him.
    Pyth. Ha! were it possible!—may he yet come!
    Cal. Into the sinews of the horse that bears him
Put swiftness, gods!—let him outrace and shame
The galloping of clouds upon the storm!
Blow breezes with him; lend every feeble aid
Unto his motion!—and thou, thrice solid earth,
Forget thy immutable fixedness—become
Under his feet like flowing water, and
Hither flow with him!
    Pyth. I have taken in
All the horizon's vast circumference
That, in the glory of the setting sun,
Opens its wide expanse, yet do I see
No signal of his coming!—Nay, 'tis likely—
Oh, no—he could not!   It is impossible!
    Cal. I say he is false! he is a murderer!
He will not come! the traitor doth prefer
Life, ignominious, dastard life!—Thou minister
Of light, and measurer of eternity
In this great purpose, stay thy going down,
Great sun, behind the confines of the world!
On yonder purple mountains make thy stand!
For while thine eye is opened on mankind,
Hope will abide within thy blessed beams—
They dare not do the murder in thy presence!

Alas! all heedless of my frantic cry,
He plunges down the precipice of Heaven.
Pythias—Oh, Pythias!

Pyth. I could have borne to die,
Unmoved, by Dionysius—but to be torn
Green from existence by the friend I loved,—
Thus from the blossoming and beauteous tree
Rent by the treachery of him I trusted!
No! no! I wrong thee, Damon, by that half thought—
Shame on the foul suspicion! he hath a wife,
And child, who cannot live on earth without him,
And Heaven has flung some obstacle in his way
To keep him back, and lets me die, who am
Lest worthy, and the fitter.

Proc. Pythias, advance!

Cal. No, no! why should he yet? It is not yet—
By all the gods, there are two minutes only!

Proc. Take a last farewell of your mistress, sir,
And look your last upon the setting sun—
And do both quickly, for your hour comes on!

Pyth.   Come here, Calanthe! closer to me yet!
[*Embraces her.*

Ah! what a cold transition it will be
From this warm touch, all full of life and beauty,
Unto the clammy mould of the deep grave!
I prithee, my Calanthe, when I am gone,
If thou shouldst e'er behold my hapless friend,
Do not upbraid him. This, my lovely one,
Is my last wish—remember it!

Cal. Hush! Hush!
Stand back there!

Pyth. Take her, you eternal gods,
Out of my arms into your own!—Befriend her!
And let her life glide on in gentleness,
For she is gentle, and doth merit it.

Cal. I think I see it—

Proc. Lead her from the scaffold!

Pyth. Arria, receive her!—yet one kiss—farewell!
Thrice—thrice farewell!—I am ready sir.

Cal. Forbear!
There is a minute left: look there! look there!
But 'tis so far off, and the evening shades
Thicken so fast, there are no other eyes
But mine can catch it—Yet, 'tis there!   I see it—
A shape as yet so vague and questionable,
'Tis nothing, just about to change and take
The faintest form of something!
   Pyth. Sweetest love!
   Dam. Your duty, officer.   *[Officer approaches her.*
   Cal. I will not quit him
Until ye prove I see it not!—no force
Till then shall separate us.
   Dam. Tear them asunder!
Arria, conduct your daughter to her home.
   Cal. Oh, send me not away—Pythias, thine arms—
Stretch out thine arms, and keep me!—see, it comes!
Barbarians!—Murderers!—Oh, yet a moment—
Yet but one pulse—one heave of breath!   Oh, heavens!
       [Swoons, and is carried away by Arria and Officers.
   Pyth. *[To the Executioner.]*   There is no pang in thy deep
      wedge of steel
After that parting.—Nay, sir, you may spare
Yourself the pains to fit me for the block.—
       [Drawing the lining of his tunic lower.
Damon, I do forgive thee!—I but ask
Some tears unto my ashes!
      [A distant shout is heard—Pythias leaps up on the scaffold.
By the gods,
A horse and horseman!—Far upon the hill,
They wave their hats, and he returns it—yet
I know him not—his horse is at the stretch!   *[A shout.*
Why should they shout as he comes on?   It is—
No!—that was too unlike—but there, now—there!
Oh, life, I scarcely dare to wish for thee;
And yet—that jutting rock has hid him from me—
No!—let it not be Damon!—he has a wife
And child!—gods!—keep him back!—   *[Shouts.*
   Damon. *[Without.]* Where is he!

PYTHIAS AT THE BLOCK.

DAMON *rushes in, and stands for a moment, looking round.*

Ha!

He is alive! untouched! Ha! ha! ha!

[Falls with an hysterical laugh—loud shouts without.

Pyth. The gods do know I could have died for him!

And yet I dared to doubt!—I dared to breathe

The half-uttered blasphemy! *[Damon is raised up.*

He faints!—How thick .

This wreath of burning moisture on his brow!

His face is black with toil, his swelling bulk

Heaves with swift pantings. Damon, my dear friend!

Damon. Where am I? Have I fallen from my horse,

That I am stunned, and on my head I feel

A weight of thickening blood?—What has befallen me?

The horrible confusion of a dream

Is yet upon my sight.—For mercy's sake,

Stay me not back—he is about to die!

Pythias, my friend! Unloose me, villains, or

You'll find the might of madness in mine arm!

[*Sees Pythias.*] Speak to me; let me hear thy voice!

Pyth. My friend!

Damon. It pierced my brain, and rushed into my heart!

There's lightning in it!—That's the scaffold—there

The block—the axe—the executioner!

And here he lives!—I have him in my soul!

[*Embraces Pythias.*] Ha! ha! ha!

Pyth. Damon!

Damon. Ha! ha!

I can but laugh!—I cannot speak to thee!

I can but play the maniac, and laugh!

Thy hand!—Oh, let me grasp thy manly hand!—

It is an honest one, and so is mine!

They are fit to clasp each other! Ha! ha! ha!

Pyth. Would that my death could have preserved thee!

Damon. Pythias,

Even in the very crisis to have come,—

To have hit the very forehead of old time!

By heavens! had I arrived an hour before

I should not feel this agony of joy—

This triumph over Dionysius!
Ha! ha!—But didst thou doubt me?   Come, thou didst—
Own it, and I'll forgive thee.
    Pyth. For a moment.
    Damon. Oh, that false slave!—Pythias, he slew my horse,
In the base thought to save me! I would have killed him,
And to a precipice was dragging him,
When, from the very brink of the abyss
I did behold a traveler afar,
Bestriding a good steed.—I rushed upon him,
Choking with desperation, and yet loud
In shrieking anguish, I commanded him
Down from his saddle; he denied me—but
Would I then be denied? As hungry tigers
Clutch their poor prey, I sprang upon his throat:
Thus, thus, I had him, Pythias! Come, your horse,
Your horse, your horse, I cried.   Ha! ha! ha!
    Dion. [*Advancing and speaking in a loud tone.*] Damon!
    Damon. [*Jumping on the scaffold.*] I am here upon the scaf-
        fold! look at me!
I am standing on my throne; as proud a one
As yon illumined mountain, where the sun
Makes his last stand; let him look on me too;
He never did behold a spectacle
More full of natural glory.   Death is—[*Shouts.*] Ha!
All Syracuse starts up upon her hills,
And lifts her hundred thousand hands. [*Shouts.*] She shouts!
Hark, how she shouts! [*Shouts.*] Oh, Dionysius!
When wert thou in thy life hailed with a peal
Of hearts and hands like that one? Shout again!   [*Shouts.*
Again! [*Shouts*] until the mountains echo you,
And the great sea joins in that mighty voice,
And old Euceladus, the Son of Earth,
Stirs in his mighty caverns. [*Shouts.*] Tell me, slaves,
Where is your tyrant?   Let me see him now;
Why stands he hence aloof?   Where is your master?
What is become of Dionysius?
I would behold, and laugh at him!

[*Dionysius advances between Damon and Pythias—Damon being on the scaffold—and throws off his disguise.*

Dion. Behold me.

Dam. and Pyth. How?

Dion. Stay your admiration for awhile,
Till I have spoken my commandment here,
Go, Damocles, and bid a herald cry
Wide through the city, from the eastern gate
Unto the most remote extremity,
That Dionysius, tyrant as he is,
Gives back his life to Damon.   [*Exit Damocles.*

Pyth. How, Dionysius?
Speak that again!

Dion. I pardon him.

Pyth. Oh, gods!
You give his life to Damon?

Dion. Life and freedom!

[*Shouts and drums. Damon staggers from the scaffold into the arms of Pythias.*

THE END.